AF472416

Deceitful Affection
A True Story

Courtney Hernandez

First Edition

ISBN: 978-0-9879832-0-6

A special thanks to Tanisha Weisner and Laura Dorman for editorial support and to Laura Dorman for her photography.

Book design by Lulu.

You taught me how to love, now teach me how to forget how it feels.
Who will heal this pain that you left inside of me?
Who ever invented love should have made instructions on how to end the suffering it causes.

"Aventura"

Dedicated to all marriages that have succeeded through immigration and to my devoted husband.

Table of Contents

Epilogue

Ms. Smith met her husband in the lobby of a beautiful Caribbean resort. He approached her with a compliment and she liked the attention. There was obvious chemistry and the two went dancing at a local discotheque night after night. She found his culture and rhythm irresistible.

Ms. Smith reluctantly returned home and soon accumulated a large Visa bill from visiting him every three months. After two years of long-distance dating, they wed in the resort where they first met. She was overjoyed thinking about the day he could finally live with her in Canada.

He landed in Toronto that December receiving his permanent-resident status, as well as a social-insurance number and a health card through his marriage.

Shortly after he arrived, he unexpectedly started picking fights. At first, Ms. Smith brushed it off thinking he was just adjusting to life in a new country. However after she refused to send money to one of his friends in need back home, her husband became surprisingly angry with her and she began to worry about their relationship.

Several days later, Ms. Smith came home from work and found all of her husband's things missing. She called his cell phone hysterically trying to find out what happened but he would hang up or only speak Spanish when he answered. She didn't know what was going on.

Increasingly frantic, she hired a private investigator in his country and unfortunately found out that the friend her husband so desperately wanted her to send money to, was his own four children and girlfriend. She spent the next few days in bed deeply depressed. She couldn't believe that she had married someone whom she obviously didn't even know.

She will never recover from the experience, especially since her husband still lives somewhere in the same city, his permanent-resident status intact.

Every winter Rhonda traveled to the same resort with her girlfriends. She was lying by the pool one day when she noticed a new animation staff member. She was intrigued by him and called him over.

"What's your name love?" she asked.

"Robert." He smiled as he approached her lounge chair.

"How long have you been working here?" She sat up to get a better look at him.

"A few months now, you must be a VIP!" he pointed to her bracelet and smiled again.

They ended up spending every possible moment together and eagerly got married a year later.

A few months after she submitted the immigration application, her husband unexpectedly lost his job.

"The hotel is slowing down and they let me go. Now I won't be able to pay my rent this month and I have no money for food."

Rhonda was deeply troubled by his situation. "Oh, baby that is awful! How much do you need for rent and food? You can look for another job until you come to Canada and then everything will be fine." She sent him the money right away.

A few days later he called her all excited. "I have a job interview this Friday at another hotel! I think I'll get the job but they do medical tests before they hire someone and I don't have money to pay for them. I asked my friend but he said no and..."

"How much?" She interrupted him. "You need a job. I miss you so much."

The next week she called him to hear more bad news.

"I am in the hospital, there was a car accident and I broke my arm. I will probably lose my job and I don't have any money to pay for the medical bill. I don't know what I am going to do. You have already helped me so much." He whined.

She felt so sorry for all his bad luck but he would be in Canada with her soon, she would just have to get him past this rough patch.

As time passed Rhonda sent him money biweekly to help him through all of his bad luck until he came to Canada.

When he finally arrived she threw a party for him and invited all of the Latin friends she knew. He liked his new circle of friends and they invited him to go downtown to the bars almost every weekend. Rhonda drove him to and from the clubs while she babysat or did other odd jobs to pay back all the dept she'd accumulated.

Their relationship changed. They grew apart as they were faced with real life. On vacation Rhonda wasn't the woman she was at home and Robert felt tricked. He had no one to turn to and not enough money to have the option to leave. Eventually he fell into the arms of another woman.

Robert was unfaithful to his wife for a year until she finally discovered his dark secret. Even though she was willing to try to stay together, he didn't love her anymore and was consumed by all the lies he had told.

Devastated, Rhonda eventually had to kick him out, humiliated at what he had done to her. They divorced months later and both tried to pick up the pieces of their lives.

Thousands of Canadians fall victim to marriage fraud every year. It's hard to know what to do next after being cheated on, used for money and manipulated for months if not years. It is difficult to find a relationship with someone in a different country when both parties honestly love each other and are not together because of the benefits that are attached. Some Canadians end up spending up to $100,000.00

on their spouses before they even come to Canada and when they arrive and receive their residency, they disappear.

The first thing that comes to mind for many is: “He only wants *a green card.*”

Is that true? Does taking a chance on love ultimately end up being the responsibility of the Canadian sponsor, the government or the immigrant?

1. Love at First Sight

It was early April 2002 and my parents decided to take the family on our first vacation outside of the Maritime Provinces.

I was 17 years old and I was very excited to travel outside of Canada for the first time, to fly for the first time and to see my first palm tree. The only expectation I had was to get an awesome tan.

My parents had two friends that were coming with us or rather we were going with them. They had been to Puerto Plata before and invited my family to go with them. If it wasn't for that we probably would never have gone to Puerto Plata at that time.

Unfortunately my sister and I had to share a room. She was fifteen years old, two years younger than me. We never got along and we weren't going to start just because we were on vacation. We agreed not to kill each other and tried to make the best of it considering we would be spending most of our time together. Our rooms were very appealing with two queen beds that were dressed with bright orange and green colours complementing the shinny reddish tiled floor. The resort was amazing and I fell in love with everything, especially the people. It's a feeling I am still unable to explain. It smelled different, made me feel different and put me in a different mindset just being there. I didn't know it at the time but this was going to turn into my second home.

The friends that came with us were not the kind to sit on the resort the whole time, which meant those two weeks were filled with new adventures each day. We went to the main road a few different times to flag down a "guagua" one of the various forms of local public transportation. I still remember the first time we got in one… Us tourists walking cautiously alongside the busy highway, a white oversized van slowed down beside us, a guy hanging out of the van's sliding door whistled and pointed at us asking if we wanted a ride. The van stopped beside us and the guy jumped out bargaining with my dad's friend Scott. Scott conveniently knew a few Spanish words and eventually we were pushed into the vehicle. To my surprise there didn't appear to be any available seats. I searched for a place to sit down but there were so many people I didn't know what to do.

"Just keep moving to the back." My sister whispered as she pushed me. After a few minutes the vehicle started making strange noises. I looked around and noticed that none of the other passengers seemed concerned. All of a sudden we stopped. Everybody started complaining but I couldn't understand what they were saying. The driver got out, opened the hood and pulled out this long white material object through a puff of smoke. I didn't know what to think and didn't have much time to contemplate because Scott hurried us out of the van as the helper boy tried to convince us to stay. You see, you don't pay until you are delivered to your destination.

Scott flagged down another guagua in a matter of seconds and we hurried in as the poor driver behind us tried to fix his problem and watched his higher paying tourists leave.
We walked freely around the city with confidence even though mostly everyone stared at us. Quite a few men approached us and offered to give us a tour around the city but Scott waved them all off saying "no gracias".

The first couple of days were wonderful and it only rained a little at night. My sister and I were under age but we met two French girls who were leaving and so they gave us their *of age* bracelets so we could get into the bars and drink. Our parents didn't mind because we were with them most of the time and they could supervise.

One night after the entertainment, we all went to the snack bar. I was waiting my turn in line when I saw him.
He was my age, tall and fit with gorgeous brown skin, long graceful fingers and a smile that could brighten up a room.
Feeling my stare, he glanced at me with his kind, dark eyes. I noticed he had the longest eye lashes I have ever seen on a man. I was love stricken. He carried on serving the other guests but I knew he noticed me. When it was my turn to order a drink my heart raced and I didn't know what I wanted.
"Make me something good." I flirted with him.
"I call it Merengue" he grinned and placed a drink on the counter in front of me. Rum, grenadine, orange juice and sprite I believe, and I liked it. His English was very limited but that only interested me more.
I spent every night from then on with him at the snack bar trying to get to know him. This turned out to be more of a challenge than I had imagined. My sister thought I was crazy coming back to our room after 2 or 3am every night but she was good enough to promise not to tell our parents which surprised me because usually we couldn't wait to get each other in trouble.

Juan worked as the bartender every night from 11pm to 7am except on Fridays. He also went to school. I couldn't understand what grade he was in but he was also on the basketball team. He explained with great difficulty that he went home from work and slept for a few hours in the mornings. He would then go to school and play basketball in the evenings either before or after having another nap because he would have to go back to work that night. His dedication to working long hours to help support his family when he was only a teenager impressed me beyond belief.

One night as I watched him mix me another merengue I fiddled with the stainless steel ring on my finger that my father had made for me while he was at work.
"I want you to have this." I pulled it off my hand and held it out for him. I wanted him to have something of mine that was important to me. He gladly took it, slid it on his index finger, smiled and looked to the

next person in line.
Later that night when the bar was mostly empty he asked me to follow him out back which I gladly did, right into a walk-in freezer. I didn't know what to expect but I was hopeful that he would kiss me.
One of his co-workers suddenly shut the door to the freezer and we stood there in silence nervously looking at each other for a few seconds enjoying the cold air.
"He must have planned this" I thought as he slowly moved closer to me and tilted his head. Our first kiss was awkward, mostly because we were locked inside a freezer. It started out innocently but it quickly became more intense. I soon felt his tongue playfully part my lips as he stepped closer, putting his arms around me pulling me tight as he passionately caressed my mouth with his. My heart started racing even faster when he tried to go further than just a kiss. I gently pushed him back.
"I want to be let out now please" I said as I fidgeted with the locked door.
He laughed it off and got his friend to open the door. I felt stupid from then on and was uneasy when he spoke Spanish with his co-workers in front of me. I wasn't sure if they were talking about me or not, so from that moment on I was determined to learn Spanish no matter what.
I wasn't comfortable with how forward he acted but I still liked him and couldn't stop spending the rest of my nights with him. It felt as if I was being drawn to him and when we were together I felt like someone else who had no problems or worries in life.
We spent most of our time kissing and holding hands because trying to have a conversation was very difficult.

On my third last night, I was starting to get upset about having to leave him.
"I leave in three days. I am going to miss you Juan." I touched his hand secretly because there were a lot of people around.
"Three more days" he repeated.
"Can I have your phone number?"
"Yes, you give me yours too?" He asked as he reached for the pen and note pad in his front pocket.
I knew I may never see him again and to think about it brought tears to my eyes. It was frustrating that we couldn't tell each other how we felt because we couldn't speak the same language. I told him he needed to learn English and I would try to learn Spanish so we could stay friends or whatever this was turning into.

I sat at a table close to the bar all night long admiring Juan as he served drinks. He sat with me when he could and when we were at a loss for words which happened a lot, he would talk with his co-workers in Spanish. I wished I knew what he was saying. It was strange to be amongst a small group of people who I didn't understand but was having a good time anyway. I went with the flow and enjoyed being there.

One of his co-workers came by around 2am that night and asked Juan if he could go to the Sports Bar on the other side of the resort to cover for him for a minute. The sports bar was closing at that time or maybe it was closed already because when we got there it was empty. "Come back here." Juan motioned for me to come behind the bar and sit with him on his lap.

We started kissing not wanting to miss a second that we had left together, or that was what I was thinking. Nevertheless, I was still somewhat taken aback when he tried to put his hand up my shirt. Looking back now I was naive for being surprised, we had spent a week together every night kissing.

I stopped his hand from wandering and kind-heartedly tried the best I could to explain that I was not going to sleep with him. I told him that I liked him too much to be another one of his tourist flings. I was sure that at that point in his life he had experienced more of that than I wanted to know, but we were also in a public place and bottom line, I was not going to sleep with him in a bar. Why risk getting caught on the job? He was disappointed and maybe even mad at my reaction and I wasn't too impressed when despite what I said, he tried to persuade me again. I stood up.

"I have to go. I'm sorry Juan. I really like you but you are working here and we may never see each other again. I can't do this right now." I turned, quickly left and didn't look back.

I was not going to be just another girl that he could have his way with and forget about the next day. The few drinks I had that night didn't help the situation, although he was probably hoping they would have.

On my second last day as I lay soaking up the sun, I still felt angry. I knew that I was leading him on and so forth but it didn't matter. I decided it would be best if I didn't call him when I returned home if he was that kind of guy.

As we ate lunch I thought about him. As we ate supper I thought about him and as we watched the show that night I started to get nervous about seeing him. My parents knew that I had a "thing" for the bartender but I wouldn't talk about it. I had no one to empty my heart out to. To make things worse, when we walked over to the snack bar after the show, Juan wasn't behind the bar. I felt so let down.

"Where is Juan?" I desperately asked the bartender on shift.

"He is on day off, what can I get you?"

"No thanks." I turned around and bumped into the person behind me as I tried to leave. I was so upset. I would have to wait a whole day to see him again. On top of that, it was my last day there.

I went to bed early that night.

Our last day arrived quickly and we did all the last minute things that most people probably do. We went to the market on the beach to spend the rest of our money, took as many pictures as possible, started packing and tipped our favourite staff members. We were leaving early the next morning and I couldn't stop thinking about what was going to happen that night. My sister and I got our last bit of sun by the pool while we reminisced about our time there.

"So the bartender?" She pried.

"What about him?"

"What is going on with you two?"

"I don't know, I like him but I don't know how it would work. I have his phone number though so we will see I guess." I reapplied more sunscreen.

Time went by way too fast, or did it? All I could think about was seeing him. And sure enough at 11pm he walked out from the back and went behind the bar to start his shift.

I was sitting with my family and some of the entertainment staff at a table and reluctantly asked my sister to get all of my drinks. I felt so shy and weird that I just couldn't go over there and face him. Eventually he came over to me.

"Why don't you come to see me?" He asked.

"Oh" I said dumbfounded. "Sorry."

He asked me to come with him and I hesitantly followed but deep down I was screaming "*Yes!*"

When we were out of ear shot from everyone else in the bar he stopped me and put his hands on my shoulders.

"Are you mad at me?" He forced out.

"I don't know." I responded.

"I sorry" He said. "I like you. Will you stay later?"

"Okay." I agreed and returned to the table where my family was easily convinced that everything was fine.

I was very pleased that he made the first move. There was something special about him and there was something inside of me that couldn't let him go. I really wanted to know what he had to say.

Scott joked with my parents about my infatuation with this young Dominican boy.

"After a few weeks back home, you will forget all about him." Scott laughed. "Don't worry" he said to my mother, "She will get over him in no time. This is just a vacation crush."

In some deep corner of my heart and as you will see, I know now that all the criticism, mean jokes and many jealous friends throughout the years is what pushed me harder to follow my heart until the end. I wanted to prove them wrong, show the world that it was more than a vacation fling, more than just puppy love, and I wanted to prove that it was possible for us to have a relationship even though it would be extremely difficult.

When everyone left the table I went over and leaned against the bar and watched Juan as he worked, so charming, but shy and composed. I sighed.

Eventually when the bar slowed down he was able to stand with me in between guests. He was very attentive and made sure my drink was always full. I remember falling for him hard all over again. At 2:00am the bar was pretty much empty so we sat at a table and ended up stealing kisses and holding hands all night long, both avoiding the fact that it was probably the last time we would ever be together.

"I am going to miss you so much" I tried not to cry.

"I miss you too." He touched my cheek "You call me yes?"

"Of course I will." I squeezed his hand.

Just before the sun came up he led me by the hand out onto the golden beach. He slowly took the silver chain from around his neck and placed it gently in my hand.

"I can't take this." I said.

"I want you to remember me." Our eyes met and he kissed me softly.

"I don't want you to go." He hugged me tightly and I started to cry as I suddenly realized that his shift was soon over.

He held me close as we spent our last minutes together watching the sun rise over the Atlantic Ocean. This was the first time I had ever seen the sun rise.

"I sorry for the other night, I wait for you." He smiled. I thought it was a thoughtful thing to say but I wasn't clear on what he meant and it wasn't worth the trouble getting him to explain.

He asked me to meet him outside the resort lobby to say goodbye so I started walking towards the entrance to see him off. He had to exit the hotel from the employee area.

As I waited for him, trying to hold back my tears, I wondered how this was going to work. We could barely understand each other and I was only 17, let alone the fact that we lived more than 2,800 kilometres away from each other.

I waited in anguish for over an hour but he never came. I finally gave up and cried quietly all the way back to my room where I woke up my sister who was angry and worried about me.

"I'm Okay." I lied, "It's nothing, go back to sleep." I climbed into bed wanting to die.

I might have slept for an hour after I finished crying. We had to get our bags together and leave the resort before 11am.

My sister and I threw everything into our suitcases when it was time and did one last sweep of the room. We dragged our luggage to the lobby saying goodbye to the animation staff as we walked by.

Our transfer arrived on time and we sadly boarded the bus and set off for the airport. I cried the whole way home. I couldn't understand why he hadn't come to say goodbye. Had he been playing me the whole time? He really seemed sincere and I couldn't imagine how he could have pretended.

My parents gave me evil and concerned glares the whole flight home, willing me to stop crying.

Why didn’t he come say goodbye? How could I have let myself get this involved and was he going to call me? My mind was racing and I couldn’t wait to find out what would happen next.

2. Second Thoughts

I felt better after a few days but still couldn't stop thinking about Juan. I had his number but I couldn't call him because of the possibility that he was just playing with me. Maybe he didn't want to put forth the effort to stay in touch. I still wore his silver chain around my neck, not wanting to forget our time together.

One evening, a week after we returned from vacation, the phone rang.

"Hello" My father answered. "Who?" he paused, "Oh. Hola Juan como estas, uno momento por favor" he said slowly with as much of an accent as he could manage, "Allison, phone." He hollered for me even though I was standing right in front of him.

I knew who it was. It was my Dominican bartender calling! I was overjoyed and surprised as I took the phone.

It was even harder to talk over the phone. We could barely have a conversation but were both happy to hear each other's voices.

"Why didn't you come to say goodbye?" I asked, still surprised that he called me in the first place.

"I did but you not there." He explained. "I wait for couple minutes and then my bus leave."

"But I waited for an hour for you. How could we have missed each other? I waited exactly where you told me to." I whined.

It was too difficult to discuss the exact details and I was getting frustrated so we dropped the subject.

"I only have couple minutes on my phone card so I call you next week?" He asked.

"How expensive is it to call me?" I had no idea but realized that it must have been a lot more for him to pay than it would've been for me. "I'll call you." I said.

"It is expensive but I want to talk to you, so no matter to me."

We called each other every week from that day on.

As the months passed I started taking private Spanish lessons from a nice Mexican lady who lived in my area and Juan started going to English classes. Our phone calls got a bit better.

Many times he would try to tell me something but I wouldn't hear him because it always sounded like he was in a small room with ten people screaming at each other. He would repeat himself, but when I still couldn't understand he would get angry and say "never mind, never mind" embarrassed because of his English. Looking back I think the majority of our conversations were telling each other how much we missed each other, a familiar vocabulary.

My mother and I had been having a very hard time living together. We fought about everything and things started getting a lot worse, I couldn't handle the stress of fighting with her anymore and listening to her tell me to get out of her house. I worked as a waitress at a small seasonal restaurant and with help from another waitress, we convinced one of the cooks to let me rent a room in his house.

My father helped me move my bed and all of my belongings a couple of days later. I moved out of my parent's house when I was eighteen years old.

In September, when I started grade twelve I decided to take some correspondence courses to be able to graduate with my class in June but not have to attend school during the second semester. I would be able to work more hours in order to save money to go visit my new boyfriend. This was what kept me going. I became a stronger more independent person because I had to get myself through grade twelve while working full time and keeping my dream alive of seeing my Spanish infatuation once again.

December came quickly and I had saved enough money to go back to the Dominican. Juan and I had discussed my visit and he insisted that I stay with his family and not at a resort by myself.

"We don't have hot water like the resorts do though, okay?" Juan told me.

"If you can live without hot water, I am sure I can too." I reassured him. I wasn't sure if it was a good idea but to have the opportunity to stay local and experience how he lived, I would never get that chance again, ever.

I booked a round trip flight for the coming February, 2003. I would have two whole weeks to spend with Juan!

I was so ecstatic that I quickly told all of my friends about my upcoming trip. Surprisingly, they were more amused than happy for me.

"I hear that you are going to the Dominican in a of couple months." One of my girlfriends smiled.

"Yes! I booked my flight to leave on the ninth of February. I can't wait."

"What resort are you going to?"

"I am staying with my boyfriend or whatever." I said casually.

"What?" she gasped.

"Yeah, I want to meet his family and it would be fun to see how he lives."

"Are you serious?" She laughed in disbelief.

Most of my friend's responses were; "He doesn't love you! Are you insane? He only wants a green card. You could get raped down there. What if you get kidnapped and are sold to the slave trade..." and so on. It got so bad that I stopped talking about him to anyone.

I kept my mind off of things by working as much as possible and doing homework. It was easier on me that way when I decided to cut my circle of friends down to a select few. I couldn't take the disapproval anymore. I was going to visit him, I had already booked my flight and I wasn't going to cancel it. The subject was very touchy from then on.

When my friends told me I would get raped, how did they really want me to respond? I was sad that they just couldn't be happy and excited for me like any friend should be.

My parents were not happy about my upcoming trip either. They were rather angry at my reckless decision. I later found out that my mother went to the police when she found out that I booked my flight. She tried to find a way to stop me from going but I was eighteen so there was nothing she could legally do.

My father however took me to the bank and co-signed for my first credit card.

"If you are going to do this I want you to have a credit card in case something happens." He looked concerned as we waited for the banking officer to return.

My dad did everything he could to try to make up for me and my mother not getting along. I knew that he didn't agree with my decision to go on this trip but he never tried to tell me that I couldn't go.

Exams started at the beginning of January, which was the same time I received *the* email. This wasn't just any email, it was from a Spanish email address and it contained a photo of a group of dark people on a beach in front of a hut like building, maybe a bar. The people looked Dominican and the message read;

"Hi Allison, I friends with Juan and he tells me about your upcoming visit. I excited to meet you. Juan has told me about you, we are good friends. We are going to do many things together. You are so pretty. I hope to see you soon.
PS: I the one in the middle of picture with hand in the air.
From Tambo"

I felt sick. Maybe I had made a mistake. Maybe I should cancel my trip, and maybe something bad would happen to me. I was scared and mad all at the same time but I told no one. I didn't want to listen to everyone chant "told you so".

I called Juan that night.

"Do you know someone named Tambo?" I asked sternly.

"No. Why, who is he?"

"I got an email today from someone named Tambo and he said that he knows you."

"I don't know anyone with that name."

"I got an email from this Tambo guy and he said that he knows you and that he wants to see me and that we are going to do things together when I get there." I said accusingly. "You don't know anything about this?" I raised my voice.

There was a pause of silence on the other end of the phone.

"I don't know what you are talking about. I promise I don't know anything about what you say, this is loco. We need to find who send

you this."
His response made me feel embarrassed for thinking he had something to do with it. He calmed me down and assured me again that he knew nothing about the email, I was so confused. If Juan didn't know anything about who could have sent the email, I didn't know how I was going to find out who did.

The next day at school I kept to myself not wanting to talk to anyone. I was stressed out about what was going to happen.
At lunch break when I was alone with my cousin and two friends (who for the most part didn't insult my situation) I couldn't hold it in any longer and started explaining what happened with the email. I told them with heartfelt emotion about how worried I was, how I couldn't cancel my flight and how Juan knew nothing about it.
"What do you think I should do?" I asked nervously. "Do you think someone here sent me the email trying to break us up? Everyone thinks I'm crazy."
After a few moments of sheer silence the three of them burst out laughing. I am talking about uncontrollable hysterical laughter. I wanted to disappear. I had lost almost all of my friends because they just didn't understand that I had met someone from a different country regardless if he was poor or not. I bet if he was from Europe somewhere, maybe France, they all would've been encouraging me to go and be dying to meet my new lover.
I sadly turned and slowly walked away with my head hung low realizing that now I had no one to confide in. I couldn't even turn to my family. I couldn't believe my friends would do this to me.

Later that day when I was on my way to class I saw my cousin walking towards me in the hallway. I couldn't even look him in the face. I turned and tried to avoid him.
"Listen, I have to tell you something." He grabbed my arm and I knew what he was going to tell me. He enjoyed making jokes at other people's expense and this one was at mine.
"I sent you that email." He said. "I made it up and found the picture online. I didn't think you would be this mad about it. I'm sorry."
I felt so betrayed. I didn't understand how they could think it was funny that I was scared and possibly in danger. I had never felt so alone. My mother didn't want me living at home, I wasn't sure who my friends were, I didn't really know this boyfriend who I was trusting with my life and now my cousin turned me into another joke.
I walked away without responding and we didn't speak for a few weeks. He was family however and it was inevitable that we talk eventually. I don't know if I will ever completely forgive him though.

I called Juan that night. I didn't want to but felt I owed it to him to let him know who had sent the email. He must have been a bit concerned, especially after I accused him of having something to do with it.

I dialed my Global phone card number followed by my pin and then dialed his number.
"Hola" Juan answered my call.
"Hi baby, it's me. How are you?"
"I'm at work, what are you doing?"
"I wanted to call before I went to bed and tell you that I found out who sent that email I told you about."
"Really? Who? Is it someone you know?"
"Actually, yeah. I'm so sorry to have thought you had something to do with it. If you only knew how mean everyone is to me because of our relationship you would not be surprised."
"Why are they being mean to you?" He sounded concerned.
"Umm, well..." I didn't know what to say. I didn't want him to feel bad. "They just don't understand us. They don't know you and so I guess they doubt your intentions."
"I don't understand." he said.
"They think you are with me because you want to leave your country and I am your way out." I simply said. It was always easier when I was blunt because when I used bigger words it always made things more complicated.
He became defensive. "That's not true I don't want to leave my country, for what, to live in the cold? Do you believe them?"
"I don't believe them, that is why I am coming to visit you, I don't care what anyone thinks. I make my own decisions."
I really didn't care what other people thought. It hurt my feelings nonetheless when they said mean things about the man I wanted to be with when they didn't even know him.
"I promise I'm not with you because of what they say. I can't leave my family."
"I know. I miss you Juan. We only have another month to wait until we see each other again. Make sure you have someone come pick me up at the airport. I will call you next week okay?" I changed the subject.
"I will pick you up. Don't worry." He laughed. "Talk to you soon. Bye."
I always felt better after I got off the phone with him. It made me forget about everyone at school telling me that he had another girlfriend and that he was just using me for a bigger plan. If they could have met him, they would have liked him, I was sure of it. I fell asleep hoping to dream about him.

Two weeks before my flight, my father came by to see me. He brought me a case of Campbell's vegetable soup and asked me if I wanted to go for a drive.
We went to Tim Hortons. I ordered a coffee and he had a Boston cream donut. We sat down at one of the tables and he asked me how I was doing. I only saw him about once a month so we always had things to talk about.

My sister had told me a few weeks before that my father was rushed to the hospital because of stomach pain. I asked him how he was feeling.
"I feel great sweetie, don't worry about me I'm tough as nails. What is new with you?"
"I leave in two weeks." I tried to hide my excitement.
"I know. Did you find a drive to the airport?" He asked.
He wasn't able to drive me because he worked nights and I had to be at the airport at 3am.
"Yes, a friend from work is going to drive me and Juan is going to pick me up when I get there. Are you are still coming to get me when I get back?"
"Of course I will sweetie." He smiled. "How is school?"
"Good, I finished all my exams and passed. I just have to finish my biology correspondence class and then I will graduate in June. I applied to college for Travel and Tourism so I should hear back from them soon." I was on track.
"That's great!" My father patted my hand. "So do you know what you will be doing when you go on your trip?" He turned serious all of a sudden.
"I am not sure exactly, but don't worry dad. I will be staying with him and his mother. I will be with his family, I will be totally fine seriously. It's not like he has his own place and we will be alone the whole time." I tried to convince him. "And I will call you as soon as I get there and give you a phone number where you can call me, and if anything happens I have my credit card. Everything will be okay dad, I promise. I'm going to be very careful. I have heard so many awful things from people lately. Believe me I am nervous but I trust Juan and I know he'll protect me."
"I know you'll be careful Allison, I am going to worry about you but you've always been mature at making your own decisions. I love you and remember that if anything happens, anything at all, you call me and I will do whatever it takes to help you. Okay?" He waited for my response.
"Yes dad." I laughed. "Let's go. I have to go to work soon, and seriously don't worry too much."
I was very happy that he'd come to see me. I needed a boost of confidence and parental love. I was scared about my upcoming journey. I was putting a lot of trust into this boy who I barely knew, who lived in a world I knew little about. The only thing that kept me sure about my decision was thinking "what if I didn't go?"
I would wonder what could have been for the rest of my life. I couldn't live with that kind of regret.

3. Culture Shock

On February 9th, 2003, a friend from work drove me to the airport to catch my 6am flight. I flew direct to Puerto Plata and during the four hour flight I nervously fidgeted, not able to sit still. My mind was racing with questions and fear of the unknown. What *were* we going to do and would I be imposing by staying at his family's house? I had no idea what to expect and I was scared. I had taken Spanish lessons for about 6 months by then and felt that I would be able to understand more of what was going on however I was in the dark about many things that were about to happen.

As I stepped outside into the warm Dominican air, I felt a sense of adventure like never before! Overwhelmed, I started searching for Juan. I hoped I would recognize him through the hundreds of tourists searching for their transfers.

I slowly made my way closer to the parking area and noticed that I was being observed by numerous onlookers, taxi drivers, venders, luggage guys and so on.

I was incredibly relieved when I finally saw Juan waving his arm in the air while manoeuvring his way through the crowd.

"Juan!" I called out.

He made his way over to me, swiftly took my bags and led me towards an old car in the parking lot. He put my suitcase in the trunk and opened the front passenger door for me.

After I got in and smiled at the driver he closed my door and climbed in through the window of the backseat (I guess the door didn't work). Juan and his friend talked the whole way while I looked out the window enjoying the sights and anticipating what was going to happen next. It took over thirty minutes to get to where he lived and I didn't say a word the whole way.

We came closer and closer to the big mountain of Puerto Plata and started up this long dirt road that was barely passable by car, in my opinion.

We stopped where there were people outside in the yard cooking stew over an open fire. Numerous children were playing in the street, several chickens were searching for food through the dusty landscape and I soon realized that everyone was staring at me. I was the only white person there, something I never experienced before but would soon grow very accustomed to.

The women outside cooking were Juan's mother and grandmother who welcomed me with a kiss on each cheek and a hug. His two younger step siblings were in the apartment arguing in front of the TV as he led me into his bedroom and shut the door, which I was thankful for. I opened my suit case and gave him the gifts I had brought: a new pair of basketball sneakers that he wanted, some good chocolate, gum

and lots of other small stuff. We were only alone for a short period of time before his mother came in and he introduced me to his sister, brother, and aunts and uncles.
After I said hi to everyone Juan shut his door again and started changing his clothes.
"I have to go to work now." He said. "I work at a different resort on the animation team. I will be back later, okay?"
Then to my surprise he left me there. I had never even thought to confirm what his work schedule would be before I came to visit him, a very stupid mistake.

The stew they were making smelled delicious. I sat down at the table, submitting to the whole situation and a big bowl was placed in front of me. I had no idea what it was and when I tried to ask I didn't understand their responses; I actually couldn't understand the majority of anything that was being said. I was told among every other comment to be careful what I ate. I felt rude but I only ate what I felt comfortable eating and then joined the children in the living room to watch TV, or rather observe my surroundings.
Juan's mother put her hand on my shoulder "Estas muy tranquilo no?" I laughed but said nothing trying to think of something to say but gave up. I was so disappointed with the language barrier. I honestly thought that with the lessons I'd been taking I would have been able to communicate more.

The apartment was a bottom unit in a building of four apartments. The living room was small with a TV, two plastic patio chairs and bunk beds to the right of the front door against the wall. The kitchen was to the left of the entrance with a table, four chairs, a small propane stove and a fridge. There were two bedrooms and a bathroom in the back. The building was made out of cement and the walls and floor were painted different shades of beige.

When we all went to bed later that evening Juan still wasn't home yet. I wanted to ask when he would be back but I didn't want to make the effort so I waited, lying in bed listening to all the different noises of the night. Motorcycles and scooters passed by continuously, stray dogs barked at each other into the night and I could hear loud music from vehicles passing by in the distance.

Juan finally arrived home around 1am and loudly brought his scooter in the living room safely along side where his mother's boyfriend's motorcycle was.
After locking the front door, he came into the bedroom. I was so relieved to be with someone who spoke English and I had so many questions, like what had I eaten for supper, what time he had to work while I was there, did he always come home this late and so on. I found out that he had to work six days a week all day long with breaks for lunch and supper. I looked at him with wide eyes and moaned in disappointment. It was going to be hard to get over the fact that I would

be spending most of my time there with his mother and not him.

We hadn't kissed yet with all the commotion and it felt awkward finally being alone together with almost no chance of being interrupted. My heart raced as he comfortably undressed down to his underwear in front of me and climbed under the sheet beside me.

"How was your day at work?" I asked and turned towards him.

"It was okay." He turned to face me.

I was so nervous I didn't know what else to say. He had already answered all of the questions I asked.

We laid there looking at each other for a few tense minutes, wondering who was going to make the first move. We didn't know each other that well considering we had a weekly phone date for almost ten months.

"Are you nervous?" He whispered.

I nodded, unable to speak.

"Can I kiss you?"

"Yes" I whispered back.

He slowly moved closer and put his arms around my waist and gently moved his lips towards mine pressing up against me softly. I felt a sense of relief that we were finally together doing what we did best, however it felt strange. I needed to get to know him more in person. He carefully started moving his hands up from my stomach as he caressed my tongue playfully with his. I was so consumed by his passion that I didn't notice when his hand was cupping my breasts all of a sudden. I quickly removed his hand.

"Not yet." I sadly looked him in the eyes. He was disappointed.

"Are you sure?" He smiled shyly.

"I'm sorry Juan, can we wait?"

"Okay." He kissed me. "Goodnight." He turned on his back but still held me close. I was grateful for his reaction.

The next morning he left early to go to work and I stayed in bed as long as possible. When I finally got up I went into the living area where his mother was cleaning the kitchen and had breakfast waiting for me on the table.

Juan's two younger step siblings were playing in front of the TV and stared at me as I sat down at the table. It was so out of body like to wake up in a Spanish home not knowing anyone, not able to speak the language but accepted and welcomed into their lives.

The sun was beaming down on the palm trees outside and I wished I was on a beach. The smell of laundry was in the air mixed with garlic and motorcycle exhaust, I love those three smells together to this day. Children outside were screaming as they chased the chickens down the road and there were people coming and going continuously carrying food items back home to prepare their lunch. I could see this all because the door was always open.

People stopped in all morning as Juan's mother finished cleaning up from breakfast and started making lunch and washing the clothes. I understood a quarter of what was going on. Some people stopped in for coffee or a drink of water, others just to talk, but I was almost positive that she had more visitors than usual that morning only because I was there, a white girl sitting by the open door.

Juan came home for lunch and told me that it was too much driving to come home twice a day and so from then on he would not be coming home for lunch. I was not pleased with his decision but nodded in response.

His mother took me shopping with her that afternoon for what she was going to make for supper that evening. She held my hand the whole way and put me in the middle of her and the moto concho driver (motorcycle taxi). She was very protective of me, yelling defensive responses at men passing by who were whistling and hissing at me. I was surprised when some of the men hollered things to me in English. I guess they made an effort to learn a few phrases for the ladies.

It turned out to be a very exciting day walking through the downtown area and taking moto conchos here and there. She also took me to a few places I wanted to go, like the bank and a corner store or colmado so I could buy some of their cheap cigarettes.

I realized that my Spanish was better than I had thought. I was being forced to speak only in Spanish the whole time and I was learning very quickly.

By the time we got back home I was tired, Juan arrived shortly afterward for supper break and again I was so thankful to be able to speak English.

"Do you want to go for a drive?" He hugged me and nestled his face into my neck. We drove around the boardwalk where the waves were quite fierce and refreshing. It was beautiful and I giggled at a motorcycle that passed us carrying two adults and three small children. We went to visit his aunt for a minute and then back home for supper before he had to go back to work.

That night was lonely. I sat in the living room watching Spanish cartoons that I didn't understand and listened to his family talk or argue. I couldn't tell the difference.

Juan arrived home late into the night again and joined me in his room after he brought his scooter into the house and locked the door. He was cool from his drive and a little drunk but I didn't mind.

I watched him undress, admiring his dark glowing skin in the moon light. He jumped into bed next to me and started kissing me tenderly. He slowly started inching farther and farther up my shirt. I took his hand in mine and kissed his fingers.

"Oh Juan" I paused, "We have barely spent any time together. I want to wait a little bit longer please." I knew I was pushing it but hell I'd only spent a few hours with him in the run of two days and felt more comfortable with his mother.

He was disappointed again but this time he grabbed a blanket and

tossed it on the cement floor.
"I will give you space until you are ready." He said calmly.
"What are you doing?" I gasped. "You can't sleep on the floor, I am just not ready to have sex with you but we can still sleep together." I was very upset.
"It is okay. I don't want to make you feel uncomfortable." He smiled but I could tell he was faking it.
I pleaded with him but he wouldn't come back to bed so eventually I gave up and felt horrible.
Looking back now I understand why he was frustrated. Maybe I was in the wrong for thinking I could stay with him and not succumb to his charm on the first night. Maybe that was why he wanted me to visit him in the first place. It took me forever to fall asleep as I wondered what I should do.

The following night when Juan came home from work I was hoping we could start over. I pretended I was sleeping and waited for him to jump in next to me but instead I heard him drop a pillow on the floor.
I quickly turned over and looked at him fiercely.
"You can't sleep there again." I waited for him to say something or climb in next to me but he was silent.
"If you are going to sleep there then I will too." I got out of bed and stood over him.
"Fine" He was defeated and slowly got up.
"I missed you today." I whispered in his ear as he lay down next to me.
"I missed you too." He said with his back to me.
I was not surprised at his cold response. The last thing he probably wanted was to get hot and bothered again only to listen to me tell him to wait. I propped myself up on my elbow and tenderly kissed his neck to lessen the tension.
He couldn't resist and turned over to face me, he looked earnestly into my blue eyes as if trying to tell me that he didn't know what to do. He caressed my face in his hands for a few serene moments as I gazed into his kind dark brown eyes and affectionately rubbed his arm. He kissed me with such passion I didn't know it was even possible to get aroused so intensely. I could hear myself breathing faster and suddenly stopped so I could listen to the sounds of the apartment. I hoped no one could hear us.
His heart beat through his chest faster and faster. I opened my eyes and saw the moonlight glistening on his damp forehead. The temperature was rising quickly.
I threw the sheet back, eagerly put my hand on his chest and started inching down feeling every individual muscle on his stomach. I was lost in the moment and the only thing I could think about was how much I wanted him. Just before I had him in my hand he excitedly grabbed my breast in his right palm and squeezed my nipple firmly as I took hold of him. I was so overwhelmed I moaned out loud and he

quickly covered my mouth with his hand.
I struggled to remove my panties and he followed my lead. We threw our clothes across the room and I swiftly rolled on top of him and little by little I lowered myself. Our eyes locked and I could see the ecstasy on his face as he watched me move up and down, the moon reflecting off my nakedness.
It was everything I had ever wanted and more, we took our time and it was worth the ten months we had waited and all the insulting things everyone had said to me.

The next few days were very repetitive. I would wake up and Juan's mother would have my breakfast on the counter waiting for me.
She worked part time as a maid at a resort so I spent a lot of time alone in the apartment. Juan's siblings went to school in the morning and when they came home in the early afternoon I had to babysit which I didn't like one bit. Maria who was eight and Luis who was five were not very well behaved children. Luis hammered nails into the concrete walls just for fun and he broke the toilet one day. I don't know how but it wouldn't flush and no one could fix it so they had to hire someone. I had to try to make them behave for my own sanity but that was hard when we couldn't speak the same language.
I couldn't understand the TV enough to watch it and I couldn't leave the yard because I didn't know where I was going and because I would be stared at by everyone in the vicinity which made me nervous.
The power would go out randomly every day and it would be gone for hours. Many times when we were all watching TV at night, Juan was at work, the power would shut off all of a sudden. That made the nights even longer as I waited for Juan to come home. Someone would light a candle and we would all sit in the living room looking at each other.
Maria used to stand behind me and play with my hair as I sat in the kitchen waiting for Juan to come home. She loved how soft it was and I enjoyed her gentle calming tugs as she braided and brushed my blond locks. I wanted so badly to tell her how much I liked it but didn't know what to say.
I asked Juan one night when he came home why the power went out all the time.
"The city doesn't have enough power to supply everyone. The government has to shut the power off in different places to make sure that everyone gets power sometimes." Juan explained.

One afternoon, I cleaned the entire kitchen and walls with a scrub brush. I was in the house all day long when it was so nice and hot outside. I regretted not staying at an all inclusive resort but then I wouldn't have been able to experience those long passionate nights in Juan's bed.
I gained a few pounds because of the large portions of food I was eating and the only time I got out was when Juan's mother took me to run errands with her or visit family members, which was fun but again, the

language barrier made it very frustrating.

One evening when Juan was home for his supper break, he was relaxing in front of the TV and I was by his side.

"Juan, can we go for a walk or something please?" I asked.

"I tired. Maybe tomorrow okay?" He didn't even look away from the TV.

I was so restless and irritated from doing nothing while in this beautiful place.

"I'm so bored though, I've sat here all day." I complained. "I really want to get out of the house and go somewhere. I am getting fat and I didn't come here to sit in an apartment by myself the whole time."

"Fine" he sighed and pulled himself away from the TV.

We went for a walk, but we started arguing more often because he had to make more of an effort to please me.

Then Juan finally had a day off. Lucky enough it was on Valentine's Day. I wanted to do something special so I asked him if we could go to a resort for the night. I was paying and he picked one that I could afford. I was thrilled to be back on a resort with hot water and power that didn't go out randomly. I was mostly excited to be able to understand what was going on and speak my own language for a day. Juan told me that his friend wanted to come along with us. He had some extra money and wanted to go. He would get his own room, of course. I wasn't very happy with the idea but Juan said they rarely had the opportunity to stay on a resort so this must have been something his friend was looking forward to. I kept my mouth shut.

We checked in at 2pm and after we dropped our bags off in our room we went and sat by the animation staff area and Juan chatted with his friends who worked there.

I was not happy that we finally had a whole day together and he wanted to partake in the daily activities.

To my surprise his friend Matteo (who could thankfully speak English) and I ended up spending most of the day together while Juan was off playing darts and socializing.

Close to the end of the afternoon Juan finally appeared. Matteo and I watched as he came walking towards us. I was mad and suddenly noticed that he was also in a rage as he walked faster and faster towards us.

"I have been looking all over for you. Where have you been?" He looked at his friend with an equal amount of anger and started yelling at him in Spanish.

"Juan what did you expect me to do while you were out playing games and talking to your friends."

"Well where have you been?" He yelled at me.

"This is the first whole day we have together and you go off with your friends ignoring me, and you are mad at me? Thank god your friend came along so I have someone to hang out with." I was furious that he would accuse us of anything other than waiting for him.

I stood up. "I don't have to put up with this." I turned and started walking. I had the room keys but I wasn't sure where I was going to go. I was annoyed and upset that he didn't follow me. He stayed behind arguing with his friend.

I walked around aimlessly for a while eventually ending up at our room. I went in, sat on the bed and started to cry.

There was a banging on the door within 5 minutes. I opened it and Juan came bursting into the room and started pacing back and forth but wouldn't say anything.

I finally broke his silent rampage "This is not working out. I thought we could spend some time together as a couple. Your friend wanted to come along and I didn't complain. Then you left me for hours and when you come back you're mad at me?" He followed me outside on the patio.

"I thought we could spend some time together too." He said more calmly. "Why didn't you come with me?"

"I am sick of not understanding what is going on. I want to speak English and I want your full attention. I paid for us to come here because I want to be with you and do things together, not with your fifteen friends who work here." I glanced at him crossly through accumulating tears and noticed that he was actually becoming livid.

"YOU paid for this! You PAID. So you think I should be at your beck and call? *I* will PAY you back, I didn't ask you to pay for this." He went back inside.

I was speechless and didn't know how to react. He took me entirely the wrong way. I realized that I had made a big mistake. I did have to pay for a lot of the things we did because he couldn't afford it but I always understood and would rather pay for us, than do nothing.

I slowly entered the room, frightened at what would happen next. He was in the bathroom with the door shut.

"Juan I am sorry, I didn't mean it like that" I said through the closed door. "I just thought that we would have some quiet time together and I could relax in English."

It took him a while but he eventually came out of the bathroom and we argued for a while before deciding to go for supper.

He was irritated the rest of the night and I began to ask myself, why am I putting up with this? Why am I doing this? Needless to say our Valentine's Day was not as special as I had wanted it to be.

The next few days were boring, hot and annoying. I brought a Spanish/English dictionary and I was learning more Spanish than I had learned in the whole six months of lessons. I was able to talk a bit more every day.

Juan's next day off, a week later, was better than the first. We went to the beach and the grocery store and he took me to clothing stores so I could do some shopping and buy some things I wanted to return home

with. He then surprised me by taking me to a cable car where we ascended to the top of Mount Isabella into the clouds.
We explored the park at the top and stopped to take pictures on a bridge; now this was romantic.
We sat down on a bench to take a break when Juan looked at me seriously and smiled "Allison, I'm so happy that you came to visit me. I'm having such a good time and I want us to stay together forever.... I love you." He said as he brought out a ring case, opened it up and showed me a beautiful engagement ring.
I was speechless and almost fell over. As a very practical person, I was in disbelief, "you can't *love* me," I responded after a minute, "We barely know each other."
We stared at each other for a few minutes desperately thinking of what to say.
I felt bad because I did care for him so much and I couldn't crush him by denying him this, I just thought we were so young.
"I want to marry you too." I paused. "I don't know if I can say I *love* you just yet but I want to stay your girlfriend and after I am finished school we will get married if everything works out. I know this is not what you wanted to hear but it's the best I can do." I smiled at him, kissed him softly and gladly slipped the ring on my finger.
"These crazy Dominicans move fast" I thought to myself.
I admired the ring as we walked back to the cable car. It was gold with a leaf like pattern all around it, and an elevated diamond in the center. It was beautiful.
We descended and went to his aunt's house. Juan's cousin who was our age (around eighteen) met us at the door. She noticed the ring right away and grabbed my hand. She pulled me over to a friend who was there and they loudly conversed about the ring. Obviously she was very surprised and excited all at once that Juan had asked me to marry him but I felt as if she was making fun of the situation because of the way she was laughing and I felt embarrassed. The problem was that she wasn't looking at me or talking directly to me. She was just holding out my hand for her friend to see and discussing it with her as if I wasn't even there.
When we left to go back to his mother's house Juan stopped on the boardwalk and we got off his scooter so we could sit and watch the sun set over the waves on the beach.
He finally sensed that something was bothering me.
"It seemed like she was making fun of me." I complained. "She was dragging me around by the finger."
"No she wasn't. She was just showing her friend the ring."
"It seemed like she was making fun. Is it because we are so young or does she think our relationship is a joke?"
"Of course not" He looked at me as if to say that was enough.
We soon went back to his mothers place for supper. We didn't eat until

10pm. They usually ate late but this was *really* late for me. We had giant hamburgers and pop in glass bottles from a street vendor, I loved it!

Time flew by and on my second last day when Juan came home for supper I asked him to take me somewhere before he had to go back to work.

"I so tired" he yawned.

"I only have one day left." I sighed. "I paid a lot of money to come here and I hate sitting around inside."

I immediately corrected myself from saying that I paid a lot and told him how much I disliked babysitting and not being able to talk to anyone. I rambled about everything that bothered me and it felt good to finally say something.

"I have to go back to work." He said and left abruptly.

I spent the rest of the night writing in my journal and thinking about whether or not I wanted to continue our relationship or not.

When he came home that night we didn't say a word to each other and I decided that I would have to end our relationship somehow. If he didn't even want to talk about our problems when we were just starting out, then so be it.

The last day of my visit finally came and I was ready to go home. We waited for his aunt to come pick us up and take me to the airport. She was late, and I had miscalculated the time it would take to get there, so when we pulled up beside the departures area I asked Juan to bring my bag and I ran to the check in counter.

"Checking in for Air Transat 216 please" I huffed.

The man behind the counter looked at me sympathetically after a few seconds on his computer, "I'm so sorry Miss but the plane is boarding right now. I'm afraid you won't be able to make it."

"What!" I cried. I was horrified. I wanted to go home more than anything.

"The next flight out leaves in three days, would you like to reserve a seat?" He looked at me but I was in shock and couldn't speak.

"The cost is $330.00 Canadian for that flight. Miss..?" He was getting impatient.

"Okay" I said quietly and started to cry.

I managed to pay for the ticket with my new credit card through my accumulating tears and take it from the clerk who didn't say another word. I cried all the way back to Juan's place where I threw myself on his bed sobbing.

"I need to call my parents." I cried.

Juan rushed off to buy a phone card because he didn't have any minutes left on his phone. I called my parents as quickly as I could and let them know what happened and asked them to call my job. I assured them that I was fine but was very annoyed that I would be late getting home.

Juan went to work and I stayed in bed all day. Juan's mother tried to get me to come out but I wouldn't. They even got one of his aunts to come over and ask me if I wanted to go shopping or something, anything to make me stop crying and come out of the room. It made me even more annoyed that she suggested shopping. I barely had enough money to buy another flight home. I was broke and sick of being nice. I held back all my anger towards every uncomfortable unhappy situation that I had been put in for the whole two weeks. I couldn't do it anymore.

When Juan got home for supper he came in the bedroom and tried to comfort me.

"I just want to go home." I sobbed. "I can't take the cold showers anymore. People won't stop starting at me everywhere I go, I am getting fat, and it is so nice outside. You work too much and don't want to take me anywhere." I buried my face in his pillow.

"Listen, I sorry you missed flight. I am happy that you're still here with me though. I know it must be hard to stay in the apartment a lot. Do you want to come eat supper with me and after we can go for a walk?" He smiled.

It took me a few minutes to compose myself but I finally got myself together and we went out to the kitchen table where his family was sympathetic and happy to see me.

After we ate we walked to the store down the road where Juan bought me some candy. He held my hand and tried his best to make me laugh but I was emotionally detached.

He went back to work and I went straight back in bed to feel sorry for myself for the rest of the night. When Juan returned home I pretended I was sleeping and he didn't disturb me.

I managed to go along shopping with Juan's mother the following morning and then I helped her cook lunch.

We spent the day together with the dictionary trying to have a conversation and made notes of things we couldn't translate to ask Juan about later when he got home. I really enjoyed the time I spent with his mother throughout my stay; she was so kind to me.

As those three days passed Juan tried really hard to make me happy. He took me out every evening and did whatever I wanted to do, he didn't complain once about being tired. I slowly changed my mind about wanting to break up with him and when the day came that I had to leave I was so upset. It was going to be painful to go back to our phone relationship and if I hadn't missed my flight, I would not have felt that way.

It was a sad drive to the airport where we said a heartfelt goodbye. The ironic thing was, when I got to the check-in counter I was advised that my flight was delayed five hours so I had to wait all by myself nervously avoiding flirtatious Latino men until I could check in.

When the counter finally opened I rushed over and unexpectedly met up with another girl who was also alone. We smiled at each other and

motioned for the other to go ahead when we both started laughing.
"No you go first." I giggled.
"Okay. Thanks. I have been waiting here all day. I didn't know the flight was delayed." She explained.
"Are you serious?" I was very interested. "I was here all day too. I didn't know either."
We ended up checking in together and I discovered that she too was there visiting her boyfriend. We had a lot in common and she didn't live very far away from me back home. Her name was Haley, she was a pretty girl; confident, with long shiny dark hair, green eyes and an athletic figure. We became friends and exchanged stories. I was grateful to have met someone else who was in the same situation. I had thought before that there could only be a very small number of people who would complicate their lives with a long distance relationship, especially with someone from a poor country. To my surprise, I soon discovered that it is rather common.

Back in Canada and missing my boyfriend, I went to school a couple of times a week to do my correspondence course and see what few friends I had left. I was seriously the talk of the entire town when people found out that I was engaged. They were all in suspense to see what was going to happen next. Everyone at school, even people I didn't know came up to me and asked to see the ring.
I thought the diamond was real for a long time until someone disagreed with me and proved me wrong. I felt really stupid when I realized that it would probably have taken him a life time of savings to be able to afford a real diamond.

Glowing with joy, I *had* come back after my courageous visit unharmed and engaged to the man of my dreams. Some of my friends actually started being happy for me and took my relationship more seriously. I wore the ring but I told everyone who gave me a dirty look that we were both too young to get married and if we did, it wouldn't be for a few years. That encouraged some of them to make fun of me even more; I couldn't wait to graduate, move away and disappear into the general population.

4. A Not So Perfect Visit

The year passed slowly and I finally graduated from high school with my class at the end of June, 2003. I was hopeful that Juan could come to Canada on a visitor's Visa and go to prom with me.

I went to the bank and sent him $500 to apply, this was the first and only time I sent him money and I had a feeling I had sent too much, but how was I to know otherwise? That is what he told me he needed.

After a few hopeful weeks Juan called and broke the news that he was denied for the Visa. I was heartbroken because I would miss the opportunity to finally introduce him to everyone, especially those who had laughed at me so many times. To this day I am not sure how much the application for the Visa truly cost him but he never asked me for money again nor did he try to tell me stories which would encourage me to send him anything. If he would have I'm not sure I would have sent him anything. I didn't have any money to give.

I started college in the fall and I began to plan my life around being with my man. He wasn't able to come to my country so I would have to go to him. I was determined to make sure that he did love me and that he wasn't with me only because he wanted to leave his country, as all my peers were so sure of.

I had kept in touch with the girl I met at the airport the year before. She was going to visit her boyfriend again for a week and asked me to go with her. So that December during the one week I had for Christmas Break, we booked our flights and made reservations at a local motel in Sosua, a town close to Puerto Plata. Haley had two other friends who were also coming along with us. I called Juan right after I booked my flight and told him about it.

He was hurt that I didn't plan on staying with him for the week but I quickly reminded him of the last time. I didn't want to pay a bunch of money to go sit in an apartment again, and besides I was going with a friend who had actually lived there before and her Spanish was exceptional.

I promised Juan that we would definitely see each other as much as possible and I asked if there was anything he wanted me to bring him, but he didn't want anything.

The four of us flew down on December 27th, 2003. I walked out of the airport and breathed in the hot humid air. I closed my eyes as I stood in the middle of a huge crowd of tourists making their way to their transfers, I was back.

Haley had her Dominican friends pick us up in a van and they were very excited to see us as we walked over to the parking lot where they were waiting for us.

"Hola Haley!" They all hugged her. "Who are your friends?" They checked us out.

"This is Allison, Sara and Jessica. Where's all the rum!" Haley jumped into the van on top of her boyfriend.

They dropped us off at our motel and we merrily went in to check out our room. It was simple, just two double beds, a small TV on a dresser, a fan and a full bathroom off to the side. There was no air conditioning or hair dryer, unlike a resort. I didn't care though nor did Haley but her two friends looked quite upset.

We dropped our bags on the floor and decided to go to a bar for a drink and get some lunch.

We walked down the street to find a place.

Half way through our meal at this open air beautiful quaint bar right on the beach, Haley's two friends who were quiet and distant the whole time finally spoke up.

"We don't like the room." They complained.

"It's fine. I thought we agreed not to go to a resort." Haley reminded them.

"Yes but that was before we saw the place we are staying at. There are bugs everywhere and it doesn't look that safe. We don't want to stay there."

"There aren't bugs everywhere, just give it a night and have an open mind. I've stayed there before and I assure you it is safe. The owner is Canadian and he knows me. Let's wait until tomorrow and see what you think then?" Haley sweetly smiled.

"We are going to the resort down the road, it's an all inclusive. We did not sign up for this." They said firmly.

Haley and I looked at each other disappointedly but at the same time relieved. We would have to pay double for the room if the two of them left because we were going to split it four ways, but if it meant that we didn't have to entertain and support the other two girls through the culture shock they were experiencing, maybe it was better that way. They returned back to the room to get their bags and we didn't see them again until the flight home.

My 19th birthday was on December 28th. After we got dressed that morning, Haley showed me where I could call Juan from a public phone center nearby.

"Why didn't you call me yesterday when you got here?" Juan sounded upset.

"I was busy getting settled, I don't have a phone and I didn't know where to make a phone call." I regretfully replied.

"I know but you could have tried. I was worried about you."

"I know baby but I am calling you now. How are you? When can I see you?" I asked.

"I am fine and I don't know. My day off is in a few days." He was annoyed.

"Okay." I said "So how do I get to you, can you come pick me up?"

"I don't know, it's far and I don't want to take my scooter. I'll have to

take a taxi. Why don't you come and stay with me for a few days?"
"Baby we already talked about this. I don't want to babysit and wait for you to get off work every day. I am here with my friend and we're going to spend most of our time on the beach."
"Fine," He pouted. "Call me tomorrow."
"Okay" I promised.

That night, we went to Haley's boyfriend's friend's place. It was right on the ocean, it was perfect. We got a big bottle of rum and made Kool-Aid and the party started.
Coincidentally, someone else in the group was also celebrating a birthday that night and we cheerfully celebrated together. There was a great variety of people there, I met two Italian brothers who were living in Sosua because their parents owned a business there and a few older English speaking foreigners from Europe.

Before we decided to go out dancing I went inside to use the bathroom. When I was coming back out I opened the bathroom door and Alex, one of the guys who picked us up at the airport was abruptly right in front of me.
"Ah!" I was startled. "Do you need to use…" I couldn't finish because he jumped towards me and planted his lips firmly on mine. I quickly pushed him off me justifying that he had had too much rum.
"Hey Alex, I have a boyfriend."
"I am not jealous." He smiled.
"A Dominican boyfriend" I continued.
"Oh. Well where is he?"
"In Puerto Plata. We have been together for over a year now. You're cool Alex, just don't try that again." I punched him firmly but playfully in the shoulder to show him that I wasn't worried about it and briskly exited the house in search of my friend. I couldn't believe that he had just kissed me so suddenly like that. "Who does that?" I laughed out loud. I had a great night and we didn't return to our motel until after 2am.

I called Juan the next morning when I got up and we had the same disappointing conversation as before. I didn't want to go stay with him until he had a day off I was having too much fun.
"I'll call you again tomorrow, promise. I miss you." I hung up.

Sosua, is very touristy with shops and restaurants everywhere, everything is within walking distance. We spent every day at the beach. Sometimes a few of the guys who surfed would come with us and we watched them play in the water, but most of the time we ended up talking about our boyfriends.
We got snacks and liquor at the grocery store every afternoon and would get a huge hamburger for supper which cost sixty Pesos, about two dollars Canadian. It was the biggest burger ever, just like the one I had when I stayed with Juan the year before.
In the afternoons we relaxed at the motel and talked to the staff before

having a shower and getting ready for the nights festivities which always included going to Haley's boyfriend's friend's house on the ocean where everyone always went. I was learning a lot of Spanish because not many of them spoke any English. I was having an incredible time.

The following day I called Juan again but this time I was growing impatient, I knew his day off was getting closer.

"Hey baby, so when can you come get me? Can you come tonight?" I missed him so much.

"I think so, maybe around six o'clock."

"Where do you want me to go?" I asked.

"I have to get out of the taxi at the main road and walk to your hotel, which one is it again?"

He had never heard of it before and decided to come around 6pm to find it. He was really annoyed throughout the whole conversation which disappointed me, I was having so much fun and he was depressing me.

That evening I waited on the street for over thirty minutes anticipating Juan's arrival and worrying about what kind of mood he would be in. Haley waited with me so that I wouldn't have to be alone. I finally saw someone walking towards me on the empty street but couldn't tell if it was Juan or not.

As he kept coming closer, walking directly towards me, I finally recognized him and started waving my arms in the air. He was wearing a bandana and I barely recognized him. I wanted to run up to him and jump in his arms like in the movies, but he was very composed and I didn't want to embarrass myself so I controlled my excitement.

After an awkward kiss, I introduced him to Haley.

We walked back to the motel to get the bag I had packed.

I showed him our room and then we left. He didn't say much of anything on the whole thirty minute ride into Puerto Plata.

To my surprise, he lived in a different place next to one of his aunts, in a gated community. His family was very happy to see me again.

It was dark when we went to his aunt's for supper where I was kissed by everyone. We sat down to eat and I actually understood a bit more than before.

"Is there anything wrong?" I asked Juan quietly when I found a moment that no one was listening.

"No."

"Well you're not really saying much to me. We haven't seen each other for a long time. I just thought you would be happier to see me, that's all." I sighed. I wasn't having as much fun as I expected.

"I am happy to see you, but we are just at my aunt's house. What do you want me to do, start kissing you in front of everyone?"

"Yeah, I wouldn't mind." I smiled.

We didn't go back over to his mother's place until midnight. As we entered his room I looked around briefly. It was empty except for his bed, a fan conveniently positioned towards his bed and a closet where his clothes were hung. It would be so simple to have very few belongings. So uncluttered, I thought.

I noticed my graduation picture was framed on the floor next to his bed and smiled. I was going to comment when he silenced me with his hand against my lips and gently pulled me down on the bed where we had our second kiss of the year.

Taking my face in both of his hands, he flexed his shoulders and pulled me into him. He tasted sweet like the Presidente we drank earlier and the faint smell of his cologne was comfortably familiar. The kiss lasted for a few wonderful seconds until he pulled away and looked at me as if to check if it was really me. He smiled and hugged me burying his face in my hair. I squeezed him back and he kissed me again, harder this time.

I painfully thought of all the nights I had spent with him on the phone wishing we were together and here he was. I didn't foresee that I would feel so uncomfortable when we were finally together but there was an unfamiliar way about him that made me nervous just like the last time I came to see him.

He removed his lips from mine and stood up pulling his shirt over his head revealing his smooth, hard, dark stomach and hairless chest.

Overcome with the longing that had built up inside of me for an insufferable ten months, I grabbed his hands and awkwardly pulled him down on top of me.

"I need you Juan." I whispered while he kissed my neck.

Goose bumps prickled over my whole body as he slipped my shirt over my head and struggled with my bra.

We explored each other's bodies like we had never been apart, but the intense desire we both felt exploding out of us demonstrated just that.

I fell asleep on his chest while rubbing his belly, admiring every part of him. It was like every element of me wanted to sink inside of him so that we would never have to be apart again. I wished time would stand still, I was so happy.

The next morning, I woke up earlier than usual. I didn't want to miss any minute of the short time we still had together.

"Morning baby" I whispered to his sleeping face.

I gently ran the back of my index finger alongside his cheek and kissed his forehead. The sun shone in through the cracks of the metal shutters as I lay next to Juan listening to the sweet song of tropical birds.

I studied my sleeping lover and gently touched his short dark curly hair, moving my hand down along his strong arm to the top of his hip. He was so stunning and my mind filled with memories from the night before. I lightly brushed my lips with his but he didn't move.

The air was humid and warm and smelled like sweet flowers. I grew

impatient waiting for him to wake up, it was his day off and I was eager to finally spend some time with him. I needed to use the bathroom but didn't feel comfortable leaving the bedroom without him. I softly made circles with my finger on his triceps hoping he would shift.
"Ummm" He groaned. "What time is it?
"I'm not sure sleepy head." I kissed him and he backed away a bit dazed.
"Let's get up." He yawned.

We got dressed and went into the kitchen for breakfast. His mother had yucca and eggs already waiting for us on the table.
It was New Year's Eve and after we ate, we hopped on his scooter and drove around to visit his family members that I hadn't seen in a year. They were all happy to see me and I got kisses from everyone. We were invited for lunch at one of his aunt's houses and then he took me to Costambar Beach.
He actually let me drive his scooter for a few daring minutes on a very quiet part of the street. That was very exciting but frightening at the same time. I was happy when Juan took control again and I was safely nestled behind him with my arms around his belly.

After parking his scooter on the beach under a walnut tree, we paid to sit in a beach chair and positioned it in the shade because Juan didn't like the sun one bit. "But I'm black" he would say.
"I finish college this summer!" I said as I looked back towards him, we were cuddled up on the one chair.
"What are you going to do after that?" He questioned.
"I don't know." I really didn't know what I was going to do but I knew why he asked. "What would you like me to do?" I smiled.
"I want to marry you." He said seriously.
"I know. I haven't decided what I am going to do but whatever that is, it will be based on that."
"Do you want to marry me?" He searched my face for an answer.
"Yes I do, it will just take a bit more time." I hoped I wasn't being too honest but I just couldn't marry him based on two visits in two years. There was still so much I didn't know about him. "Tell me about your childhood." I smiled and lay back down against him.

After an hour or so on the beach, Juan was getting restless so we left and drove to the Malecon and sat on the railings of the boardwalk. I held his hand and we sat in silence for a few minutes watching a fisherman far out on the coral reefs.
He took my left hand in his and kissed my engagement ring.
"I love you." He said.
I smiled. "I am really sorry that I didn't stay with you, I wish you could've gotten the week off from work."
"You know I can't. We only get vacation when the hotel slows down."
"I'll try to come see you when I finish college this summer in August, eight months from now. I am going to miss you so much."

I got up and straddled him, looked into his sad eyes and hugged him. It was getting late in the day and we soon would have to go. It was painful thinking that I had to leave him all over again.
I pushed myself off of his chest a little bit so I could look him in the eyes and as I started to tear up I said "I love you" for the first time. He was so relieved and happy to finally hear me say it that I could almost see tears in his eyes as well.
"I love you too Allison. We have made it this far, I think we'll be okay. I told you that I wait. You will be my wife some day."
As he kissed me I knew that he was right. I would be his wife some day.
"We have to go." He got up and brushed the sand off his pants. "You want to drive?" He laughed.

We had supper waiting for us back at his mother's house and after we ate, I said goodbye to his family.
We started walking in search of a motoconcho and then a guagua to get back to Sosua. I held his hand tightly, wishing I would have stayed with him regardless of the consequences.
As we arrived at the motel and entered my room, we unexpectedly found Haley and her boyfriend there. I immediately felt like we were interrupting something as they both looked either embarrassed or upset. Either way, I knew something was wrong.
After some quick introductions they left us alone so that we could say our goodbyes.
"I feel really bad that it is New Year's Eve and we can't spend it together." I complained.
"I work tonight. It's one of the busiest nights of the year. I already told you." He explained again.
"But we are going to miss the midnight kiss and we are in the same country." I hugged him tightly not wanting to let him go. It wasn't right that we were actually in the same country but we couldn't be together. It was mostly my fault. I sighed.
I tried to hold back my tears as I promised to call him the next day.
He left and he didn't look back.

That night, Haley and I, along with a bunch of friends went to Cabarete to celebrate. It was the first time I had ever been there and I was in awe. A long stretch of beach maybe a couple of miles long, with restaurants and bars lined up along the whole shore line. It was beautiful.
"How do we decide which bar to go to?" I laughed.
As it got closer to midnight, the beach turned into a massive party. As I watched the fireworks I wondered what Juan was doing at that second and I felt miserable when I noticed that everyone around me was kissing. I looked up at the gleaming moon and hoped that he was also looking there as I did all the time back in Canada. It was, after all, the same moon. It was a small way I could feel that we were together in the

world.

When the excitement died down and we were all feeling tipsy we flagged down a taxi and drove back to the motel. As we approached the gate to enter, I noticed that it was closed and we were locked out. I started to panic.

"Holy shit!" I grabbed the lock. "How are we going to get in?"

"Don't have a fit. I know where the key is." Haley smiled at me. "He leaves it out for me when I ask."

"Well maybe we should go somewhere else for a drink before we go to bed. I just sobered up imagining us being molested while passed out on the street." I was serious.

She ignored me and removed the padlock.

We stumbled to our room where we fell asleep instantly.

We woke up on our last day earlier than we had planned.

"My head" I moaned through my hands.

We forced each other out of bed and slowly put our beach clothes on. We went in search for breakfast and then I called Juan from the phone center.

"I will come back to see you as soon as I can and I will stay with you next time." I promised.

"You'd better stay with me." Juan said seriously.

"We fly back home tomorrow at noon. I will call you when I arrive?" I said.

"I will wait for your call, I miss you." Juan replied.

On the beach with big bottles of warm water we wondered how Haley's friends enjoyed their vacation.

"Where is your boyfriend?" I asked Haley. "It's our last day and he isn't with you."

"Remember when you walked in on us with Juan. Well we broke up." She hid her face in her hands.

"What? Why?" I put my hand on her shoulder empathetically.

"I found out that he has been cheating on me. He has another girlfriend in Europe somewhere." She struggled to hold back her tears.

"How could he do that to you?" I was shocked, but then remembered that long distance relationships are so hard. "It is his loss. He doesn't deserve you." I gave her a sympathetic squeeze.

"It's not fair. I come down to see him a few times a year. I tried so hard to make him happy. I did whatever he wanted and he has been cheating on me, playing us both at the same time. I don't know for how long, and the other girl probably has no clue either." She drank deeply from one of our warm bottles of water and spit some out over her feet.

I didn't know what to say. I felt awful and it probably made her feel worse that I was still happy with my boyfriend. I started wondering if Juan had any other girlfriends. If he did there was no way for me to find out, I could only visit him once a year. I forced those thoughts out of my head and tried to support my broken hearted friend. Our last day was a sad one that was for sure.

The next morning the sun was beaming down on us as we were brought to the airport by the same gang who picked us up, Haley's boyfriend decided to come as well. He spent the whole ride there trying to convince her that he wasn't cheating on her, I was disgusted.

As we flew home we listened to songs from the Dominican group Aventura the whole way, which made us even more depressed than we already were.

I had a great vacation but started worrying about my relationship with Juan. Did he have another girlfriend? I was confused as to what the future would bring.

5. This Is It!

I finished college at the end of July 2004. Juan and I had consistently called each other at least once a week after I returned home from my second visit. We both were very eager to see each other again. I had done a lot of research about moving to the Dominican in the meantime and I had found a picturesque apartment complex off the beaten path by a river in Puerto Plata. The pictures on the website looked nice so I contacted the owner who was Canadian.

I reserved a furnished bachelor apartment for the end of August for $100 USD per month. I was very excited and managed to keep this a secret from Juan. I wanted to surprise him and at the same time show him that I was independent.

I was fortunate to be able to move to the Dominican to be with him. I didn't want to get married after only a few times being with him on vacation and then try to get to know each other afterwards. I had prepared my life for this. I was finished my schooling, I had no real responsibilities and nothing was holding me back from moving wherever I wanted.

I carefully packed all the things I couldn't live without and things I wasn't sure if I could get in the Dominican and said a heartfelt goodbye to my family. I gave my father an extra long hug because he had recently found out that he had developed diabetes because of a terrible accident he experienced in his early twenties that had made him lose most of his pancreas and liver. He wasn't following his diet properly and he drank as much alcohol as he wanted, despite the consequences. I was worried about him and told him to smarten up if he wanted to live long enough to see me get married.

I flew into Puerto Plata for the fourth time on August 28th, 2004, and I was greeted by the owner of my new apartment who was holding a sign with my name on it. She was tall and skinny with dark golden sun kissed skin.

I followed her to a rusty blue pickup truck in the parking lot and after we put my suitcase in the back we started driving towards my new home.

To my surprise the apartments she owned were back a long dirt road. It was very quiet, beautiful and private but also very far away from everything and very hard to get public transportation from.

I was disappointed but tried to stay positive.

When we finally arrived she introduced me to her Haitian helper who took my bags. I followed close behind him as he led the way to my apartment.

My new place was on the second floor of a two unit building. It contained a double bed, a small table with two chairs, a small fridge in the corner and a kitchen sink with a few unfinished cupboards below.

What surprised me the most was the bathroom! In the back corner of the square room there was a wall separating the bathroom area and the door was a shower curtain. I moved the curtain aside to look behind it and I saw that the area was elevated from the floor by one step. The toilet had a shower head right above it. So you could literally use the bathroom while showering at the same time, I laughed to myself.

My escort left me to unpack and it was so hot that I decided to try out my new shower.

The cold water was a shock to my system and I chuckled, realizing that this was only the beginning of many cold showers to come. I tried not to trip over the toilet that was in my way as I turned the water off and moved the shower curtain aside.

As I stepped down out of the shower into a puddle of water, I realized that I had just flooded my apartment. The drain must not have been working and all of the water had run down from the bathroom and all over the floor.

I franticly searched for a broom, a trick I learned from Juan's mother, and found it behind the entrance door. It took me a while to sweep all the water outside. Luckily for me, I hadn't emptied my suitcase out onto the floor.

After I got dressed, I took some time to settle in for a little bit and then went back down to my landlord's apartment and she took me to the city to get groceries, a phone card, toiletries and anything else I needed.

When we got back home, she let me use her phone to call Juan. Boy was he going to be surprised! I trembled as I dialed his number.

"Hi, Juan' I said nonchalantly.

"Hi honey" Juan said.

"How are you doing? How is the weather?" I asked smiling to myself.

"It's okay, what are you doing?" He sounded suspicious and I realized he must have had caller ID and noticed that I was calling from a local number.

"Nothing, I am at work. Where are you?" He questioned.

"Well baby, I'm in Puerto Plata!" I shrieked through the phone. "What time do you get off?"

"What? Where?" He didn't sound as surprised as I had wanted him to be.

"I'm in Muñoz. I rented an apartment here. I want to see you." I said proudly still trying to impress him.

"I will come when I get off work." He said. "I think I know where you are."

While I waited for him, I went down to the river to explore my new backyard. I introduced myself to some other Canadian tourists who were also living there. Some only spoke French so we couldn't really communicate but I met one girl from Ontario who was only a few years older than me. We became friends instantly. Her name was Emily. She was a bit shorter than me with dirty blond hair and pretty blue eyes. She gladly showed me around the property, how and where to do my laundry and she also warned me about tarantulas. She also told me not to go outside alone at night. She was happy living there and told me that I would be too.

"What made you come here?" I asked her.

"I was taking international business in university and part of the program is going to a foreign country for a term of school to learn the language. I picked here and ended up staying longer than I planned. I have a boyfriend here."

"Yeah, I totally understand." I laughed.

Juan finally showed up a few hours later when my new friend and I were having a game of pool close to the main building. He looked older and also a bit irritated, he didn't seem very happy to see me at all.

I introduced him to Emily and then he followed me to my new apartment.

"Why did you do this?" He said when we were safely inside.

"What are you talking about?" I gasped.

"Moving here without telling me... You shouldn't have done this."

"I wanted to surprise you baby. Aren't you happy that I'm finally here?"

"Yes but I wish you would have told me. This is really far away."

"Do you want to make some supper?" I asked trying to change the subject.

I was almost right across from where he worked only back a dirt road. I didn't think it was as far as he was making it out to be and I was hurt that he wasn't even pretending to be excited.

"No, I have to go home. My mom doesn't know where I am."

I couldn't believe that he was going to leave me after all I had gone through to be with him. I started to feel embarrassed that I hadn't told him but I never imagined he would be angry with me. I was, however, still firm on not being totally dependent on him and wanted to build a normal relationship where we dated and did not live together right away.

For a second, I wondered if he had another girlfriend and the fact that I had showed up unannounced might have made things difficult for him. Could that be why he wasn't excited? My heart throbbed. It was a lonely first night in my new home and I hoped that would change, I had expected him to stay with me. I couldn't sleep all night.

On my second day in the DR, I woke up early and called Juan from my landlord's phone. He was at work but only for the morning as he had surprisingly asked for the afternoon off to spend with me.

He came to pick me up around noon and took me to buy a cell phone and to visit his family for a bit. They were all happy to see me and I could finally understand more of what was going on with my now three years of Spanish lessons and lots of studying.

To my surprise, everyone seemed to be unhappy with where I was living. I didn't see their point. It was far away but it was beautiful, there were other foreigners who lived there, the river was very nice to swim in and they had a community pig roast every Sunday. I thought it was great and brushed off their concerns.

That afternoon Juan and I went back to my place and cooked our first meal together. He did most of the cooking because I was unsure of how to cook plantains and how to use a propane stove.

He seemed happier than before and agreed to go swimming with me in the river. We were the only ones there and it was hard to keep our hands to ourselves as we sat in the shallow cool water and flirted with each other.

Afterwards we had a few games of pool with two other Dominicans who lived there. At that time, I thought my choice of apartment was great, Juan seemed happy and we were having a few beers. I wish I could go back to that night, we were both so young and in love, it was so exciting.

To my relief, Juan stayed with me that night. As we climbed the stairs to my apartment, I was excited to feel his smooth dark skin on mine. As I locked the door our eyes met and we both smiled.

We woke up early the next day because Juan had to go to work.
I kissed him goodbye at the door and watched as he drove away.
I sighed with happiness as I started unpacking some more of my things. When my apartment was looking like home to me, I ventured down to the river and thankfully found Emily.

We spent the day together talking about life in the Dominican. She was very fluent in Spanish but her boyfriend couldn't speak any English. She had found a job as a waitress at a touristy restaurant and was enjoying life. I admired her.

Juan came to visit me on his supper break and told me that he wasn't able to spend the night because his mother didn't like him driving down that long road in the dark. I was disappointed but couldn't argue with what his mother said so we made supper together and then I watched him drive away again as I held back my tears. So far my life in the DR was not what I had hoped it to be.

I hid in my apartment for a while thinking that I had made a mistake by not planning my move in with him, things would've been different if we had a place together.

I eventually wandered outside in search of Emily and found her playing pool with her boyfriend.

"Hey, what are you guys doing tonight?" I asked hoping that she wasn't doing anything so I could talk to her about Juan.

"We are going to a dance up the road at this bar later." She smiled. "Do you want to come?"

"Ahh, I don't know, Juan is working and I don't want to be a third wheel." I replied.

"Who cares, it is a great time, and we will find you someone to dance with!"
I wasn't sure it was a good idea but I didn't want to sit in my small room alone all night, especially if the power went out.

Around 10pm the three of us walked five minutes up the road to an open aired bar with no walls. It only had a ceiling and a cement floor. The music was so loud that we had to scream in order to hear each other. It was a party!
We each got a beer, found a table and that was where I sat all night. I didn't want to dance with anyone, even though Emily tried to get me to dance with a number of her boyfriends' friends, I enjoyed watching everyone else. I had never seen such skilled dancing. I noticed that mostly everyone was a very dark color and when I mentioned it to Emily she told me that we were at a Haitian bar, the community that lived on this road was Haitian.
We had a great time and didn't go home until after midnight.
I went to bed right away and hugged my pillow tightly wishing Juan was there with me as I tried to fall asleep.

The next day Juan came to see me on his lunch break. We walked up the road to a small colmado to buy some eggs and made lunch while listening to Los Negrs, Tu Eres Mi Reina, on the stereo I had brought. We ate on the stairs outside my door in the hot sunshine while he played with my new cell phone.
When the music stopped playing we ventured down to sit by the river and relax before he had to leave me and go back to work.
"Can you stay tonight please?" I asked.
"I don't know. I'll call you later tonight and let you know if my mom is okay with it."
I was frustrated that he was nineteen years old and had to ask permission from his mother for everything, or was he using that as an excuse. I'm not sure why I wasn't more frantic about my suspicions, I guess I saw my situation as an experience that I wanted to have. If he did have another girlfriend, he would have to choose quickly because I had arrived. I wasn't half way across the world anymore and so if there was someone else, I would find out.

Later that evening around 9pm Juan called me as I was getting ready for bed.
"Can you come to the plaza? I have some friends I want you to meet."
"I don't know. There is no transportation here after dark." I was disappointed.
"Can you ask someone to drive you?"
"I don't know." I truly wanted to go but I had no idea if it was possible. "I will ask my landlord if she knows anyone and I will call you back."
I rushed over to her apartment and knocked on the gate rails outside. Her Haitian helper came to the door, noticed me standing there and then disappeared. My landlord appeared quickly afterwards and I told her

my predicament.
"You could go over to the cab drivers house up the street; it's the second house on the left. If he is still awake he might take you for an increased price." She suggested.
I got my friend Emily to come with me because I was scared to go anywhere alone in the dark.
The light was on in his home but I felt bad as I knocked on his closed door which probably meant that he was going to bed soon.
It took a few minutes but he finally opened the door and agreed to drive me with some hesitation but after all, he was charging me triple the price. I hurried back to my apartment to get ready and then returned to the cab driver's house where he was dressed and starting his car.

By the time I arrived at the plaza it was 10:30pm and I had to wait thirty minutes until Juan got off work.
I met him at the side entrance to the plaza shopping center where the staff bus stop was and I noticed that he was alone.
"Where are these friends you wanted me to meet?" I asked
"They are coming. We are going to meet them at Hemmingway's."
"Okay." I grabbed his hand and kissed him.

We got a table outside the bar and ordered a drink. It was a very warm night. Cigarette smoke filled the sweet air and the bar was packed with tourists from all around the world. There were quite a few tables outside which all had green umbrellas and four chairs that were all occupied.
After our drinks Juan led me inside. The cool air conditioning surrounded us as we past the lively dance floor in between the line up at the bar and he sat me down at a table that was filled with people I didn't recognize.
By this time, Juan had a few drinks in him; he usually had a few at work before his shift ended.
"This is Sara. This is Rose, John, and Elizabeth…" He introduced me to everyone at the table and I noticed they were all German speaking. Juan exchanged a few more words with them in German.
I smiled and all of the sudden he left me there by myself. I was furiously surprised.
"How are you tonight?" One of the girls asked me with a German accent.
We made small talk while I tried to locate Juan out of the corner of my eye but I couldn't see him and after a few minutes of uncomfortable small talk, I got up and told them I would be right back.
I scanned the bar but he was nowhere to be seen, I was confused and went outside to look for him.
I finally found him by a table with two other girls. They stared at me as I approached, as if they were telling me to stay away.
"Why did you leave me there like that?" I asked him ignoring the girls at the table. "They don't even speak English." I added.

"Sorry, let's go." He grabbed my hand and tugged me away.
As he pulled me away from the bar one of the girls at the table spoke up. "You should have seen who he was with last night." She hollered with a British accent.
I turned around and glared at her. "What?"
"And the girl before that didn't even have teeth, you should have seen her." She challenged me.
I looked at Juan. "What is she talking about?"
"She is lying." He said angrily and tugged my arm again.
I looked back and snapped. "Well he was with *me* last night and the night before that and honestly, if he could have *me* I highly doubt he would be with someone who has no teeth!"
He wasn't really with me the night before but he was the night before that and I sensed that she must have been lying when she said he was with someone who had no teeth. I just couldn't understand why she would lie and try to cause problems between us when I had never seen her before in my life.
The girl stood up defensively and took a large strong step towards me. I stumbled back as Juan stepped in between us. She was a big girl and definitely could have overpowered me.
"He was with *me* the night before that. Was he with you *then*?" She viciously smiled at me and then looked Juan up and down greedily.
"This is bullshit." I growled and forcefully turned away freeing my arm from Juan's grasp.
She jumped towards me but Juan got in the way and held her back as I fled the scene. I heard her and Juan fighting behind me as I walked faster, scared of what would happen if she got past Juan. A few minutes later Juan caught up to me, grabbed my arm and turned me towards him.
"What is going on?" I demanded as I again pulled my arm out of his grasp and stood my ground.
"She is lying! Don't you believe me?" He was drunk and I was feeling my liquor as well but not as much as he was.
I looked back to where the two girls were sitting and I noticed we had attracted quite a crowd, there was a large group standing around probably waiting for a fight.
"I don't know what to think, that girl almost hit me and I have never seen her before in my life. What do you want me to think?" I yelled at him.
"She is lying, I'm telling you!" He yelled back at me and started dragging me away from the bar.
He was hurting my arm and continued yelling at me while forcefully pulling me away.
"I can't believe you don't believe me. Do you honestly think I would be with someone who has no teeth? Do you believe that I was with that fat cow as well?"

"You're hurting my arm." I cried.
He let me go but continued yelling at me. That is when I started bawling.
"I have been here for like three days. I can't believe this is happening. Why are you treating me like this? I didn't say that I believe her. I don't believe her but why would she say that?" I sobbed.
One of Juan's friends came over to my rescue and tried to comfort me. He put his arms around my shoulders and turned me away from Juan.
"Don't cry, it will be okay" He hugged me. "Juan what do you think you are doing to your girlfriend? You're being an asshole, look at yourself." He waved his hand in the air accusingly at the crowd that had gathered and started leading me away from the plaza.
I was crying so hard that I couldn't breathe normally, I felt so humiliated.
I thanked his friend in between sobs, tore myself away from him and started running towards the road which led around the complex. I heard Juan and his friend arguing behind me but I didn't care, I didn't look back and continued running away from the bar and away from Juan.
I was devastated that I had changed my whole life to be with him and after only a few days and he was acting like a mad man who cared more about defending his own reputation rather than his girlfriend.
I had no idea how I was going to get back to my apartment.
I cried as I stumbled down the sidewalk aimlessly regretting ever having come to the Dominican and asking myself if I had made the biggest mistake of my life.
"Maybe he is cheating on me" I thought as tears streamed down my face.
Juan was following me and he soon caught up. "Where are you going?"
"Anywhere but with you" I cried. "Why don't you go back with your friends and leave me alone."
"I'm sorry. I am an ass. Come back to the bar with me."
"Are you insane?" I yelled at him. "Yeah *sure* I will go back to the bar with you and cry at the table. Everyone can stare at me and wonder what you did to me. Maybe your other girlfriend will come back and beat me up, I am not going anywhere with you." I said harshly.
"Where are you going to go?" He asked with a hint of sarcasm in his voice. He knew I had nowhere to go and no way to get there.
"I don't know." I sobbed.
He came closer to comfort me.
"Get away from me." I screamed.
Juan continued following me and I eventually sat down on the grass under a palm tree, completely exhausted. He sat next to me and listened to me cry for a while. He knew he had done wrong and had nothing else to say.
It took me a long time to regain control of my breathing and he eventually explained the best he could that she was a tourist staying on

the resort he worked at and that she liked him. He promised that he had never been with her or anyone who had no teeth and that she was insanely jealous of me and probably trying to break us up so that she might have a chance.

I quickly snapped back at him "Well she is doing a great job considering the way you reacted."

We ended up going back to my apartment together at 3am.

We drove in silence and then dragged his scooter up the stairs into my apartment. Without saying a word we both fell asleep.

In the morning, Juan cooked breakfast and picked me a small bouquet of tropical flowers from the yard. He apologized over and over. I was mentally in denial about everything and emotionless to his efforts.

He went to work and left me with my thoughts. I kept going over the events of the night before in my head and just couldn't make sense of it. It took me a long time to get over what happened but I had to give him another chance. I had come all this way and fought for more than two years to be with him, I had no other choice but to see what happened, right?

As the days turned into weeks, I relaxed and got used to living in the lush jungle of palm trees, time seemed not to exist. There was a mother and daughter from Quebec living under me and I spent time with them at the river. There was also a woman that worked at the Canadian embassy who lived there, as well as a German lady who I got to know. It was very interesting to hear each person's story of why they were living in Puerto Plata.

Juan used to pick me up most evenings before he went back to work around 7pm and dropped me off at the tourist shopping plaza where I would have power and something to do. I walked around looking at different shops and sometimes had a beer at one of the small, less expensive bars. Eventually, after about two weeks, some of the people who sold excursions in the plaza started noticing me, I didn't wear the resort bracelet that tagged you as a tourist and I had been there for a while wandering around in the evenings all by myself.

A young Dominican who was at one of the numerous tour booths started talking to me and asked me what I was doing in the Dominican. His English was very good and after he found out I was living there, he offered me a job at his booth.

I agreed, it wasn't like I was doing anything else. The job was Monday to Friday from 9am to 5pm, I had to try to sell the tours to people who walked by. The catch was I only made commission, so if I didn't sell anything I made no money. I thought I would give it a try.

I worked one whole week, Monday to Friday and paid a taxi both ways as well as bought my lunch every day. It was really hard to sell the tours. I hated being harassed by pushy sales people and so I didn't want to harass other people. Unfortunately, unless you were pushy, you

didn't have much of a chance to sell anything when there were twenty other sales people who had years of experience selling the same thing, trying to make a living as well.
I only sold one tour the whole week to some lady who approached me and told me she had bought the same tour the year before from my booth so she was back to buy it again.
I think I would have made $20 commission for the week but I quit. I explained to the guy that the job wasn't for me and I was paying more to show up than I was making. I even gave him the commission I made from the one tour because I couldn't be bothered to chase it.
He said if I ever wanted to come back, I was welcome but I was done with sales, or so I thought.

One night after Juan got off work I met him outside the plaza and we started driving back to my place. We didn't even get half way down the dark dirt road with no street lights when his scooter shut off. He tried to start it but it wouldn't turn over and he started to panic and got really angry, he was scared.
We ran the whole way to my apartment while pushing his scooter. He kept repeating himself yelling at me, "Why did you have to move to this place? Why in the middle of the woods, you are so stupid!"
I felt horrible, but the fact was I knew it wasn't my fault that his scooter broke down and he was yelling at me, calling me stupid and my feet were bleeding from running in sandals, I got angrier with every step.
When we finally got to the apartment we dragged his scooter up to the second floor, brought it inside, locked the door and I started to cry.
He didn't even say goodnight.

In the morning Juan left extra early to go to work after he finally got his scooter running. I'm not sure how he did it but it wasn't anything major which made me look down at my injured feet with rage as I noticed they were still bleeding from my frightening run the night before.

He called me that afternoon and told me I had to move or he wouldn't be able to visit me very often. I had only been there for three weeks however I knew he was probably right, so I swallowed my pride and told him to find us a place.
My friend Emily had recently returned to Canada for a week's visit and when she came back to the Dominican she had moved to the city.
When she came back to the countryside to visit her boyfriend, she told me about the building she moved to and how much she liked it.
We decided to move there as well.
My landlord agreed to take me and all my belongings to my new apartment in the city.

Our new place was cute. It was in a squared blue and white painted complex with around twenty bachelor and one bedroom units. There was only one apartment available at the time we inquired that had a kitchen. We were lucky. It was a small bachelor with a queen bed, a small plastic table with two plastic chairs right inside the entrance, separated small rooms for the toilet and shower to my relief, and a small kitchen area with a fridge and a two burner portable stove that hooked up to a propane tank which we had to buy.

We could only fit about four people inside the apartment comfortably and even then it was crowded. The entrance was a sliding glass patio door with a gate that slid over and locked for extra security and there was a guard who stood watch by the main entrance at night.

The owner of the building was also Canadian, from Ontario but he didn't live on site. My rent was around $125.00 Canadian a month or 3500 Pesos.

There was a courtyard in the center of the complex with an empty pool that I asked about when we signed the lease. They said they were going to fill it up soon which made me excited, however we soon found out that the pool had been empty for years and it would probably stay that way. Many of our neighbours were single mothers who prostituted in order to support their children which made me sad and edgy at the same time, I had never seen a prostitute before.

We were quickly referred to by all of our neighbours as the honeymooners because our apartment was in the center of the complex and was the only unit that had a patio door. I enjoyed our new nickname and smiled whenever I heard it.

Emily lived across the courtyard and the German lady who used to live in the jungle with us had also moved in a week after I did.

There were also two Dominicans living there who had lived in the United States for some time so they spoke English too. I was really happy to have people to speak English with especially because I was unemployed, bored when Juan was at work and nervous to leave the complex alone.

Luckily the grocery store was right behind the building. There was also a park down the hill towards the boulevard, a few restaurants, and an ice cream shop. Conveniently, there was an internet center and a Scotiabank up the street and if you wanted a moto concho taxi you simply had to walk outside.

His family was so happy that we were only a few minutes away and they could stop by to visit whenever they wanted.

"I so happy you move!" One of Juan's aunts practiced her English with me.

The culture shock was harder to deal with than I had expected. I didn't have hot water and I didn't enjoy the cold showers. I would shut the patio door, turn off the ceiling fan and jump up and down until I started to sweat. When I was good and hot I would jump in the shower to lessen the shock of the cool water.

We also lost power mostly every evening. The majority of the time it would shut off at 8 or 9pm and not come back on until 1am or later. We would have power all night until around 9 or 10am the next morning and it would be gone again until after lunch around 1pm or 2pm. After that it would stay on until later that evening, but sometimes that pattern wasn't reliable and it depended on what part of the city you were in. We lost power for two whole weeks once because the owner of the building didn't pay the power bill.

I left him a few angry messages trying to get a hold of him; I was paying my bills, why wasn't he?

During those two weeks without power I got an infection from the water we brought in from the tap outside to bathe with. That was our only means of water for those two weeks and we were lucky to have a tap that gave us water at all when the power was off. We stored it in a large bucket in the shower space and bathed with a smaller bucket which we used to dump the water over our heads.

There are so many parasites and bacteria in the Caribbean compared to where I was from. It made me really sad that many people who live in hot countries sometimes don't have the proper means of cleanliness.

I never got used to the cockroaches or spiders. Thankfully there were fewer spiders in the city compared to the woods where I had first stayed because I have always been terrified of them no matter how big. There were times when I woke up in the morning and there would be a cockroach or two swimming around in the toilet, or when I went to the kitchen to make breakfast, a roach would run down the kitchen sink drain. We started plugging the sink when we weren't using it and we had to make sure the toilet seat cover was down at night to prevent them from creeping into our apartment.

My scariest experience up until that time was when Juan was at work and the power was off as usual during the late evening. I was reading by candle light when I heard something flying around inside, it sounded like a very large bug.

I got up with the candle and tried to see what was going on when I was hit in the head. I started panicking and when I finally swatted something big out of my hair, it landed right in front of me. It was a huge cockroach. They can fly!

It recovered quickly from the fall and started flying around again, joined by another one. I started screaming and hysterically opened my door to escape.

No one came to my rescue as I nervously stood outside my apartment waiting for someone to help me. Juan always took care of me in situations like that but he wouldn't be home for a while.

I eventually had to gather enough courage to go back in with my shoe in hand and prepared myself to hunt them down and squash them.

Another hard thing for me was that I was so far away from home and when Juan and I got into arguments I had nowhere to go. He could jump on his scooter and go wherever he wanted; he could go talk to his mother or drive to a bar and meet some friends. I had to stay in the apartment with no place to go and no one to talk to. This was one of the hardest things I had to deal with; being completely powerless.

It was very relaxing to not work for such a long period of time. I had kept a job ever since I turned sixteen; not having anywhere to be for a few months was pleasantly boring.

Many days I would sit outside tanning and reading some of the books I had brought, or stare off at the sky and question if it was actually real, was I really living in the Caribbean?

I checked my email every few days and cleaned to keep occupied. Sometimes I would go across the street and spend a half an hour in the grocery store just browsing and enjoying the different products they sold. When Juan came home from work most evenings he would help me cook supper or he would take me out somewhere nice. We went to the movies occasionally, I liked going to Spanish movies even if there were no subtitles.

I was slowly adapting and becoming Dominican. I had the face twitch down as well as the attitude and all the slang sayings and expressions that were popular. Juan thought I was hilarious and I loved making him laugh. We had so much fun together and I was confident about our future together.

I ate something strange one afternoon from a small portable street vendor when we were out having a few drinks. I was wary about eating what looked like chicken liver, but Juan and his friend Felix looked like they were enjoying it and I was a little tipsy so I had some too. About three hours later I was throwing up and on the toilet for twelve hours straight. It was horrible; they said I had an amoeba. That was the first time in my life I was sick for that long from eating something. Believe me, it makes you feel like you are going to die, especially when it is 30 degrees Celsius and the only comfort you have is a small ceiling fan if the power is even on.

I got sick another time from drinking juice from a street vendor; Juan said the ice must have been bad or maybe the water. I was so exhausted from being sick and so desperate to have the comforts from back home. I checked us in to a resort for the night that time. Juan picked one in Sosua because his friend Felix worked there. He knew I wouldn't be up to watching the entertainment or having any drinks so he wanted to party with his friends.

After we ate supper I went straight back to my comfortable air conditioned room where I could take a shower with warm water and not dread the power going off in the middle of a TV program.

Juan came back to the room and woke me up around 3am that night, which made me kind of upset. It would have been nice if he would have spent more of the night with me because I was so sick.

We went home the next day and fortunately I felt a lot better.

I went to the bank to get some money for groceries that afternoon and realized that I was running out of money and fast.

"Great" I said aloud. "What am I going to do now?"

6. Life in Puerto Plata

I purposely took Travel and Tourism in school to secure a better chance of getting a job in the Dominican. I always wanted to be a hotel representative for a tour operator but you have to be hired for that job in the home country of whichever company, and then posted elsewhere. I didn't know what kind of job I would end up with but I knew I wanted to work in the travel industry with tourists.

Juan drove me around to all the tour operators in Puerto Plata and I distributed my resume to as many companies as I could.

I had been living there for a little more than two months, Juan worked every day and I sat in the apartment twiddling my thumbs, trying to be productive and wondering what to do next.

"It is time to start working" I told myself as we drove from company to company.

One hot and sunny afternoon, I was home alone as usual and I decided to go for a walk on the boulevard. This took a lot of patience because I had to put up with men hissing and whistling at me which was uplifting for a short period of time but after a while I wanted to scream "take a god damn picture would you!"

Many of the women would also gawk at me but with disgust on their faces. I felt like they hated me because I was a blond, white girl with blue eyes and they all thought of me as a threat, like I was there to take all their men away from them. I was getting used to it though and accepted things for what they were.

I left my apartment and power walked for almost an hour before I turned around. On my way back I crossed paths with a group of students in uniform that were three or four years younger than me.

I overheard one of them speaking English and I looked around. I could always hear when someone spoke English around me; I was drawn to it like a child to its mother's call.

One of the boys noticed me "Hi, how are you?" He said.

"Good." I smiled. I hoped he didn't think I was flirting with him as he was quite a bit younger than I was. "Where did you learn English?" I asked.

"In the States, I'm from Florida but staying with my grandmother for a year."

"Do you like living here?" I asked.

"Yeah, I guess. It's different" He chuckled.

"Yeah, like not having hot water." I laughed. It was fun to talk to someone who knew how different it really was to live in a third world country.

"My grandmother has one of those big black tanks that catches rain water on her roof so we get warm water most of the time." He smiled.

I was jealous and amused. I had no idea people did that and wished I

had one of whatever he was talking about.
One of the girls in the group was standing beside him listening to us. She asked him where I was from and if I was going to school there. She couldn't speak English but I could speak enough Spanish to answer her questions myself. After I chatted with them in Spanish for a few minutes she asked me for my number which I thought was strange but a friendly gesture so I gave it to her. She seemed like a nice girl and I didn't want to see disappointment on her face if I said no. I didn't have to answer my phone anyway. Looking back I can now see how naive I was.

My phone rang the next day and I didn't recognize the number. I thought it might be a job interview so I answered.
I was annoyed to hear her voice on the other end. She asked me if I wanted to hang out.
I was very hesitant but after I looked around my empty apartment and remembered how bored I was, I thought why not? I had nothing better to do so I met her in the park down the street and we walked back to my apartment.

We sat outside and I asked one of the English speaking Dominicans who lived there to sit with us because I didn't feel comfortable. He agreed to translate if I needed help but he ended up being impressed at how much I knew. I didn't need his help at all, I was proud of myself.
She asked me if she could see my apartment.
I was cautious but couldn't think of a reason to say no so we walked around the corner and went inside.
She looked around and asked if I had any jewellery.
I knew what she was getting at but I stupidly brought it out anyway. Her eyes lit up. I didn't have anything of value and gave her a few things I didn't want anymore. She then noticed that I had a belly ring because I had a few in my jewellery box and she asked if I would show her.
I lifted my shirt and she touched it gently, rubbing it between her fingers playfully, the way she looked at me and everything about the situation made me feel like she was coming on to me.
"Vamanos" I said and put my jewellery away.
I quickly ushered her outside and locked my door.
"There is a party this Saturday night." She said in Spanish as we went back to where we were sitting before.
"I don't like going out after dark." I responded feeling foolish for ever meeting her in the first place. "And my Dominican boyfriend wouldn't let me go anyway." I added knowing that would be the end of that conversation.
She was disappointed and I tried to think of something else to say but Juan arrived to my relief and I rushed over to meet him.
"Drive her home please." I begged quietly in English.
I introduced her to Juan and he conveniently offered to drive her home.

She said she would call me the next day just to make sure I didn't want to go to the party.
I waved sweetly as they drove away while wondering why I let myself get involved.

Juan returned back home and helped me cook supper. "Where did you meet her?" He was dying to know. "And what party was she talking about?"
I told him how we met and that she invited me to a party on the boulevard but assured him I would not be going. I then told him about her wanting to see our place and my jewellery.
"And you brought it right out didn't you?" He gave me an obnoxious look. "Stop making friends with just anyone. You can't trust every person you meet on the street you know. You have to remember that you are a *white* girl with blond hair and blue eyes. You are a target for all sorts of people wanting all sorts of different things. Promise me you'll be more careful. You're not in Canada anymore."
I knew he was right but I had a hard time being judgmental towards everyone, especially because I didn't have many friends.
I started realizing that I would have to toughen up and think twice before talking to strangers.
I never answered her calls again.

A month passed until I finally had a job interview with a small tour operator. They offered me a job as a representative, selling excursions in the resorts. I was so excited! It was exactly what I wanted to do. The only obstacle was that I had to get my Dominican Residence because I would be handling large amounts of money.

Juan came with me and we took the Caribe Tours bus to Santo Domingo (four hours each way) to the embassy.
I paid one thousand Canadian dollars, got my blood tested for aids and other diseases, peed in a cup and returned back home.
Weeks passed while I waited and wondered about when I would get approved, and then finally I got the call.
I had to go all the way back to Santo Domingo and pick up my temporary residence card.
Thankfully I started my new job shortly afterwards.

There was a group of twelve of us in training and I was the only foreigner in the group. It was the best training ever!
We had to go on almost every excursion or tour the company sold. Every day for about two weeks we did a different excursion and I had a blast! We went on safaris, white water rafting, city tours, cigar factory tours, a catamaran, and a waterfall hike. I got to see the country and experience many things.
After we did all of the tours, we had to spend a couple of weeks in a classroom learning how to sell them and how to do transfers with tourists to and from the airport as well as hold welcome meetings for groups of people.

We were then placed at a resort to sell tours. I swore to never do sales again but this job was kind of easy because the tourists came to me specifically to buy tours, I didn't have to draw them in. I got to eat lunch at the resort's buffet which was awesome, however it was not easy sitting behind a desk while watching all the tourists play in the pool or tan in the hot sun. I wasn't on vacation but oh how I wanted to be.

One day as I was sitting at the tour desk reading another book, waiting and hoping that someone would come buy a tour from me, I was pleasantly surprised.

"You are Harvey's daughter aren't' you?" I heard a male voice. I perked up because that was my father's name! I looked around and saw my cousin and some other people from back home standing there smiling at me.

"What are you doing here?" I said without thinking. "Oh yeah, you're on vacation!" I jumped up and down reaching out my arms, getting ready to hug them all.

They stayed and talked to me for a while asking all the obvious questions about my new life and I offered to take them to the city to show them around.

We planned an afternoon outing.

I met them at the lobby of their resort a couple of days later. We walked to the main road and jumped into a guagua that was on route for my apartment.

Unfortunately, Juan was working so I couldn't introduce them to my fiancé but after I showed them my small living quarters we set off on foot towards the downtown core. There were some children that started following us asking for money. This was normal for me, but it made my group of tourists quite upset.

"I think we want to go back to the resort now." My cousin said. "I can't handle this anymore. How can it not bother you to see so much poverty? And the dogs are just a sin, please take us back?"

"I understand." I stopped. "Let's walk back towards my place and we can get a taxi. I felt the same way the first time I came here but this is just the way it is. You get used to it I guess."

When I had them safely back to the lobby of their resort, they asked me to come back later that night to have a few drinks with them.

I liked the idea, "That would be great! You can meet Juan! How about I will talk to Juan tonight and then see you tomorrow at the tour desk and let you know." I hugged them goodbye.

That evening I told Juan about my cousins wanting us to spend the evening with them on the resort and he agreed that we should go.

We had to pay for a night pass to get on the resort which was quite expensive for us but I missed home and my family.

Time flew by as we ate supper at the buffet and watched the entertainment; it was nice to have drinks made for us. We went dancing at the resort's disco and then had a few drinks in their rooms as we caught up on the gossip from back home.

Juan and I had to leave at 1am to go back home when our night pass expired. I felt sad as I hugged them all goodnight and left the safety of the resort gates to return to my small apartment where we wouldn't have power.

Juan and I both had Fridays off. I told my boss when I started working for him that I needed to have that day specifically because it was already Juan's day off.

Every Friday was laundry day; we would rent a washing machine for 150 Pesos or five dollars Canadian.

A guy would come in the morning with the machine tied to his motorcycle and drop it off at our door. He collected the money and we started right away filling it up with water. It was the kind of machine my grandmother used to have, half of the machine was where you poured the water and added your clothes and detergent, and the other half was the spinner which rang the water out. We hung our clothes up wherever we could outside to dry.

When we were done with the machine, there were many times that our neighbours would come over and ask if they could use it. It was a good deal for them because we never asked for any money as I was the *rich* white girl.

We locked the machine up in our apartment at night and the guy came back in the morning the next day to pick it up.

On Friday afternoons we hung out with Juan's best friend Felix, and his American girlfriend Cara who was an English school teacher in Sosua. The four of us would all get together and go to the beach, play pool at a sports bar, go shopping or just relax somewhere.

Many times the boys would tell us they were going down the street for a little bit to have one game of cards or dominos and that they would be right back. Cara and I would sit outside my apartment in the sun and gossip about life.

After an hour we started expecting the boys to come back but they rarely ever did.

"They must be winning" I said as I dialed Juan's number to ask how much longer they would be.

"He isn't answering." Cara said as she called Felix at the same time.

"What a surprise, Juan's phone is off too."

This was a Friday ritual for them. They were best friends and only got to see each other on Fridays. Cara and I would not agree to stay home alone all day while they went out on our only day off too, so they would trick us to get their own way. When they did come back it was always an argument between all of us.

After we made up we would go out for supper and then to a discotheque until the wee hours of the night.

I recall one Friday afternoon especially.

"We are going to go down the road for a minute but we'll be right back." Juan said as he grabbed his keys.
"We will be right back" Felix echoed.
"We don't believe you." We both said. "Where are you going?"
"Just down the road."
"And you will be right back? Do you promise?" I asked doubtingly.
"We promise." They both looked at each other and nodded as they left.
After an hour when Cara and I were bored and hot, we called them and their phones were off. I was so sick of them pulling that one on us.
I smiled at Cara deviously. "We are going to a bar for a drink and we're not going to answer our phones."
She was hesitant but I was always angrier than she was and had more spunk. She agreed but made us wait another thirty minutes before we hopped on a moto concho and left.

We stopped for a sandwich at a small cafeteria and then crossed the street to the bar that we went to quite often.
The calls started soon after we were finished our first drink, first to her phone and then to mine. I finally answered after the sixth time Juan called.
"Hello." I said.
"Where are you?" Juan asked frustrated.
"We will be right back." I laughed. "I have to go. I'll call you back." I hung up.
To show them that we were serious, we shut off our phones.

After an hour or so, we shockingly saw them both park their scooters on the road beside the bar and smile triumphantly. They had found us. They casually walked up to our table, sat down and simultaneously slipped teddy bears out from under their shirts. They held hearts with the letters printed 'I Love You' on them.
"I am sorry baby." Was all they had to say. There was nothing else they really could say. We were only doing what they had done to us.
"How do you feel?" I asked.
"Okay. We get it, we understand. Let's leave it alone." Juan said firmly.
"Alright, but from now on I'm not going to sit around and wait for you. I will enjoy my day off with or without you." I said.

We went to a disco called *La Barrica* that night where it was so dark inside, the waiters and door men held flashlights to help us see where we were going. I didn't particularly like this club because I couldn't see anything. I heard that people had sex right there at the tables hidden by the darkness and I believed it. Unless there was a light nearby, you couldn't see the people around you, and the strobe light which was spinning at full force made things even more confusing.
It was an experience but I was happy when we left and stepped outside into the warm air, my ears rang for a while but I could finally see.

After we went out clubbing we would always go to the same small cafeteria for soup around 2am. I loved that place and ordered the same

chicken soup and loaded it up with hot sauce every time.
I hugged Juan from behind as we drove up the road towards the soup place.
Up ahead, we unexpectedly saw a number of stopped vehicles in the middle of the road. There were no police in sight as we approached the crowd and slowed down.
All of a sudden we saw a man lying in the middle of the road with his leg detached at the knee; the street was covered in blood. The other part of his leg lay a few feet from his body and he wasn't moving.
More people were gathering and I heard a police siren in the distance. One brave man carefully picked up the bottom half of his leg and carefully laid it closer to his body. The accident must have happened seconds before we arrived.
Juan sobered up instantly and turned around. The shock of seeing something like that made us lose our appetites. We drove straight home in silence. I had never been exposed to anything like that in my life and I will never forget it.

I spoke to my family once a week, I would call and get them to call me right back. I missed them a lot, especially when mom told me that my father was in the hospital again. He was in and out of the hospital at least once a year at that time.
I told mom to give him a kiss for me and informed her that I hoped to know soon if and when we were going to get married.
She was happy to hear that and told me that dad was doing okay.

I checked my email one afternoon and had received a message from my college teacher. She told me there was a group of twenty or so people in her class that year and that they were going to take their Familiarization trip that year to Puerto Plata. When I was in her class we went to Cuba which I wasn't too happy about.
She told me when they were coming and to what resort. She hoped we could meet up and I was excited to see her.

I went to the resort the day they all flew in. I was allowed to go into any resort that my company had a rep in as long as I stayed close to the tour desk.
I quickly spotted my teacher by the pool and went over to give her a big hug. She introduced me to a few of her students that were in the area and then she asked if we could meet by the tour desk in thirty minutes so she could introduce me to the majority of her group. We all gathered and I happily answered their questions about why I was living there and how it had come about as well as how I got my job.
"You are so lucky to live in such a beautiful place, I wish I lived here." One of the girls in the group smiled at me.
I offered to take them to my apartment to show them where I lived as well as to the city to show them around and go shopping. They were all extremely interested and we agreed on a day.

I asked my friend Emily to help me because the group was too big for me to keep track of by myself. It was a big responsibility for me to make sure I kept the group safe and all together.

We met them in the lobby of their resort that Friday.
We all walked from their resort to the main road, I was in the lead with fifteen people following me. A few cab drivers slowed down as we walked out of the complex and asked if we needed a drive but we all said no.
When we got to the main road there was a guagua stopped with the letter C in the windshield which meant it was on a route but it was empty so I rushed over to the driver.
"Where are you going?" He asked as he noticed the large group of tourists following me.
"Can you take all of us to Parque Tropical?" I asked in Spanish.
He jumped inside his vehicle and pulled the letter C down off the dash.
"At your service!" He smiled.
Out of the corner of my eye as I was bargaining with the guagua driver on the price, I saw my group patiently waiting for me while pointing and smiling at the busy highway traffic.
"Okay, let's go!" I waved my arm motioning for them to get in the van.
All of a sudden this man came rushing over to me and the guagua driver and interrupted our conversation.
"What are you doing?" He yelled at us in Spanish as my group quickly entered the van. He yelled at the guagua driver but I couldn't fully understand what was going on.
As the last person entered the vehicle I looked at the guagua driver with a confused and worried look on my face.
He pushed the angry man back and cheerfully told me to get in while offering me his hand.
I did as I was told and quickly sat down as the driver closed the door on the angry man's face. I was very confused and looked to Emily for an explanation of what just happened. She told me quietly in Spanish that the man was an angry cab driver that was trying to get our business.
I was somewhat concerned but we were safely on our way to my apartment and we would walk from there so I tried to forget about it.

The guagua stopped right outside of my gate and I thanked the driver for helping me out by canceling his route to take all of us.
I paid him and then led my group around the corner to my apartment.
Everyone took turns going inside because only a few of them could fit at the same time. They were all very shocked at how small it was and at what I had to live without. I didn't have any appliances like a microwave, or a toaster. I had no furniture other than the plastic patio table and chairs and to top it all off, the power was out.
Everyone was having a great time looking around the grounds and as I stood outside I tried to decide the best way to walk downtown.

To my surprise I noticed something weird out of the corner of my eye. I turned my glance and saw the same angry man parked outside my apartment building slouched down in the front of his vehicle, talking into a radio.

"Oh my god." I gasped. "That cab driver followed us here." I tried to calm myself as I couldn't let my group of tourists find out that I was worried about something.

I quietly told Emily what I saw and we decided to take the one way street that led downtown, we couldn't be followed any further if we took that road.

I led the way and Emily stayed at the back making sure everyone was accounted for. I kept looking over my shoulder paranoid of seeing the cab driver but he was nowhere in sight.

Everyone had a great time and when they were all tired of shopping they asked me to take them back.

I flagged down a large empty van taxi that agreed to fit all seventeen of us inside and after we agreed on a price we crammed in. We couldn't even shut the van's sliding door because there wasn't enough room so we all held on to each other as we tried to hold the door shut as we drove back.

The van stopped at the lobby of the resort, the group thanked Emily and I, and we all said goodbye.

"What a day!" I laughed as Emily and I got a drive back out to the main road.

"What are you doing tonight?" I asked Emily hoping that I could take her out for supper to thank her for her assistance.

"I have to work in an hour." She responded as she looked at her phone.

The van stopped to pick up another girl who was walking to the main road; it looked like she just got off work.

We thanked the driver when we were dropped off and as soon as we closed the door we were surrounded by Politour, which are tourist police.

They stopped us as well as the other lady who was getting a ride.

"Come with us." They ordered in Spanish.

I was scared and confused. Were we in trouble, why did they want to talk to us and what was going to happen? That was when I saw the angry cab driver striding toward us. He assured the Politour that the third woman (who was also freaking out and asking what was going on) didn't have anything to do with it.

"Oh my god. What did we do?" I asked Emily.

"I don't know." She said with an equal amount of fear in her voice.

The two police officers made us sit in their small office at the end of the tourist complex while the cab driver explained what had happened. I couldn't speak enough Spanish to fully understand what was going on but Emily could.

After the officers were finished talking to the cab driver they came inside and started questioning us.

"Just don't say anything." Emily whispered. "I'll do the talking."

I was so grateful while I listened and understood Emily as she told the officers that we took our friends to my apartment and to the downtown area shopping.

"Why didn't you take a cab?" They questioned her.

"Because a cab costs like thirty dollars for four people and we all got a guagua for about five dollars. Our friends also wanted to experience the real Dominican." She defended us.

"You know it is illegal to give tours without a license?" One of the officers asked as I started feeling weak.

I heard enough to know that we were potentially in serious trouble. If we couldn't convince them that we didn't do anything wrong they might take us to jail. I almost started crying.

"They are our friends who are here on vacation." Emily pleaded. "We took them to my apartment to show them where we live, we know them. We aren't tour guides."

"Wait here." They ordered.

I was so terrified that I had to use the bathroom.

I had two hundred USD in my pocket because I charged each person that came on my tour. I charged them less than the actual tour which they could have bought from the hotels but if they searched me and found the money I would look guilty of what they were accusing me of.

"Is there a bathroom?" I asked one of the officers after thirty minutes of imagining the worst that could happen.

He pointed to a door and I got up and went inside the bathroom. I felt sick with fear and my stomach was doing flip flops.

I sat on the toilet and rocked back and forth trying to stay calm. When I was finished I felt a bit better and pressed on the handle to flush. I was horrified when nothing happened.

They must not have power I panicked. I stood there for a few embarrassing moments but when I realized there was nothing I could do, I rejoined my friend in the small office and sat down beside her.

"You were in there for a while, are you okay?" Emily asked.

"Yeah, I just felt so sick. I can't believe this is happening."

"We just have to stay calm." She put her hand on my shoulder for a second.

"What are we waiting for?" I asked.

"I think they called the chief of the police and are waiting for him to come here." She calmly responded.

"Do you think they are going to put us in jail?" I nervously asked thinking of the times Juan told me he was thrown in jail for almost no reason at all.

"It's going to be ok. I just don't want to be late for work." She looked at her phone again.

"Well, I wasn't going to tell you but... they can eat my shit!" I laughed rebelliously.
"What are you talking about?"
"The toilet won't flush." I whispered. "This is insane; can they make us wait here without telling us why?" I was scared, slightly embarrassed and becoming angry.
"It's the Dominican, I'm sure they can do whatever they want." Emily sighed.
My phone started vibrating. It was Juan calling. I was late coming home and he was probably worried about me. I held the phone tightly for a few seconds deciding if I should answer it or not.
"Hello." I finally answered.
"Where are you? Why aren't you home from work yet baby?" Juan asked.
"Ummm... well, I am.....running a bit late. I will be home soon okay?" I stalled.
"Okay, I miss you. Hurry up. I will have supper ready for you." He ended the call.
"I am going to call my boss and tell him that I'm going to be late for work." Emily said as she dialed a number on her phone.
I listened as she told her boss that she would be late and then she started explaining why.
She was smiling when she hung up her phone which confused me and I stared at her.
"My boss also works for, or is affiliated with the Canadian Embassy. He is on his way here right now. He said that we do have rights and they can't just do whatever they want with us." She smiled.
I was so relieved that I almost jumped up and hugged her but we had to stay calm and collective or the officers would become suspicious.

Her boss stormed into the office ten minutes later demanding to know what was going on.
The officers explained to him that they had to wait for the chief, so we all waited.

After a while I heard some commotion outside and broke into a cold sweat as a burly man strolled into the office with his chest puffed out and glared at us two small white girls as we sat obediently on the bench. It was definitely the chief and a bunch of men rushed in the small office and started talking all at once.
Emily and I stayed seated as we listened to them argue and waited for someone to finally turn the conversation on us.
"I pay for a license to be a tour guide and she has taken my business away from me." The cab driver raised his fist towards me.
"I see." The chief agreed as numerous other cab drivers cheered.
"I have many tourists come to my restaurant every day." Emily's boss said after a few minutes of arguing that I didn't understand. "I will give

commission to any cab driver who brings people to my restaurant." He puffed out his chest.
"How much?" One of the cab drivers raised his voice over the uproar.
Emily and I were lost in the midst of this big discussion about the cab drivers and how they could make more money and what they could do to get more business.
The chief of police eventually looked at us and motioned for us to leave as he listened to the group of rowdy men argue.
We got out of there as quick as possible and we didn't look back. We rushed past the place where we usually flagged down a moto and kept on walking to make sure we were out of sight completely.
I hugged Emily and thanked her over and over for calling her boss to our rescue. If it wasn't for him I'm not sure what would have happened.

When I finally got home I explained to Juan the day's events.
"They just kept us sitting in the police office for two hours and when the chief finally arrived it was a big fight between all of the cab drivers and we were forgotten about." I complained. "I can't believe they didn't say even one word to us after they made us wait."
"Why didn't you tell me where you were?" Juan was really concerned.
"I couldn't have told you where I was. There was nothing you could do and the last thing I wanted to happen was for you to show up all worried and mad and make things worse." I hugged him. "I am so happy that it is all over. Let's get a big bottle of rum. I need a drink."

Time went on and our relationship grew through the good times and the bad. We loved hard and we fought hard.
One day Juan came home from work and was acting weird. He was being quieter than usual.
"What's the matter?" I asked.
"Well..." he hesitated "there is this girl at my resort. She comes every year and we are good friends. I usually take her to the city shopping or where ever she wants to go." He paused "Well, she asked me if I would take her to Santiago tonight to a dance club."
He could tell I didn't like the idea right away from the look on my face. It was as if he just slapped me.
He continued trying to convince me by explaining that among her outings with *my* boyfriend she would take him and his friend to the casino and give them money so they could play while they waited for her and after she would take them out for drinks.
I fought with myself because I was so jealous but realized this girl might have just wanted to experience the real culture and people of the Dominican just like I did. However, after years of her spending time with Juan and his friend she must have been attracted to one of them and obviously I assumed it had to be Juan.
"She just wants to go out dancing." He tried to reassure me.
"I don't care. She must like you. Santiago is over an hour drive away, why wasn't I invited?" I questioned.

"She doesn't know you and then she wouldn't have anyone to dance with." Juan said as I got angrier.
"Exactly, she wants you all to herself for the night. Does she even know that you have a girlfriend? How do you plan on getting home?"
"She wants to get a motel, but I told her that we have to get separate rooms, and yes I told her about you." Juan said.
"Yeah, right!" I was surprised that he was really considering going out with another woman for the night. "Have you slept with her?" I asked accusingly.
"What! No. Honestly." He stepped towards me.
"It seems like you made up your mind to go" I said calmly and pushed him back. "If you go, I will be so mad, I will never forgive you. How would you feel if I told you that I would be taking a man friend partying overnight to a city that is over an hour away, but we would get our *own rooms.* Would *that* be okay with you?"
He gave me a funny look "I guess not, but we have been friends for a long time and I take her out every year when she comes on vacation. We are just friends."
"I don't want to talk about this anymore. If you don't come home tonight after work I, I....... I don't know what I will do." I stammered and fumed as I finished making super.
I realized that this girl posed a threat to me. I was really scared that he might not come home to me that night and all I could think about was what if they were more than just friends? Was he telling the truth? Maybe he had slept with her in the past if they've always hung out so much. I was in disbelief that he would even consider taking this other girl somewhere now that I was there living with him.

He left for work after we ate supper and I was light headed from the stress of wondering what he was going to do. Maybe he hadn't slept with her.
I tried to convince myself that if he did, he would've felt guilty and hopefully wouldn't have even thought about asking me this.
I had no one to talk to and was powerless to the outcome of his actions. What if he didn't come home?
"I would have to pack my bags and leave him for good" I thought as I quietly cried myself to sleep.

7. Setting the Date

I woke up at 1am later that night to the sound of our metal gate opening which meant that Juan was home. He got off around 11pm but I was silent as he entered the apartment. I didn't want to push him too hard by asking him why he was late. I was just happy that he chose to come home rather than take a dangerous chance on our relationship.

I pretended to be asleep as he climbed in bed next to me. I wanted to question him but knew it would be best if I thought about what I was going to say first and then asked him in the morning.

We were madly in love but sometimes that isn't enough. It doesn't make people have more in common or agree with each other more often. I came to find out that we didn't have as much in common as I thought we did.

Dominican men are very dominant and it is customary for the woman to cook all of the meals, do all of the house work, the laundry, and take care of the children while the man relaxes from his day at work. It was old fashioned.

I am very down to earth but I am also very liberal in the sense that I feel all responsibilities should be shared.

We didn't see eye to eye with many things so I told him "if you want to marry someone who will do all the chores then maybe you should marry a Dominican, I'm not your mother."

"Oh no, I understand. I see how the men treat their American women at the hotel. I know it is different in your country and I will try to treat you like that." Juan told me.

After six months in Puerto Plata, February 2005 approached quickly and I had thought long and hard, taking everything into consideration of whether or not we were compatible enough to get married and live happily ever after. I wasn't too sure about the happily ever after part but I felt that if we had come all this way, we couldn't give up now.

There were things we definitely had to work on but I knew that I wanted to be with him and he wanted to be with me long term and someday have a family together.

I also wanted my life to be different. I wasn't satisfied with the idea of marrying someone from my home town, starting a family and striving for a white picket fence. I was drawn to the unknown and the excitement of being with Juan. If I married him it meant that I would have two cultures in my life, two languages and two different countries to call home. Our children would have the best of both worlds and I felt that the future was filled with so many interesting possibilities.

We went out for supper one evening and I decided that it was as good of a time as any to give him my final decision about our relationship and surprise him.

We ordered our food and after some small talk we sat back and

observed out surroundings for a minute.
I took a big mouthful of the beer I had ordered and paused to collect my thoughts.
"Juan" I smiled at him "I have thought a lot about our relationship and I want to marry you." I kissed him and swiftly got down on my knee and took his hand. "Will you marry me?"
"Get up" he whispered crossly. "You're not the one who is supposed to propose." He looked around embarrassed. "Of course I will marry you though." He said shyly as I sat back down in my chair.
I quite often did crazy spontaneous things that always embarrassed him which made me laugh at how uptight he was.
"Well if I am not allowed to propose, I shall wait for one." I winked at him playfully. "The last time you proposed was two years ago and we barely knew each other. Now that we are more serious maybe we should make it more official." I smiled bashfully.
I was twenty years old and felt that I was too young to be getting married but I had no other choice if I wanted to be with him. I was getting very frustrated with living there and knew I would soon have to go back home. The standards and quality of life there was so different from what I was used to. Customer service was nonexistent in most places, and if you were white you pretty much had to pay more for everything if the prices weren't listed. I wasn't as happy with my job anymore either, it was getting very competitive and stressful, but oh how I was going to miss the weather.

Over the next few weeks we had to plan a date for our wedding. I called my parents and let them know we were going to get married. I'm not sure if they were happy, relieved or worried about the decision but they decided that April would be a good time for them. I also asked my mother to find a lawyer who could help me with the long immigration process and told her that I would keep her updated.

I wanted to get married on a resort but we found out that we would have to pay an additional $60 per person for non guests. That meant we would have to pay for every one of Juan's family members that were going to attend; it was out of the question.
Thankfully Juan's aunt knew someone who owned a small Victorian styled open air restaurant that catered to parties and events, so we set up a meeting with her at the restaurant.
It was beautiful. Hidden from the road by enormous trees, the building was a pretty green with white trim. There was a deck surrounding the place that must have contained the kitchen and most likely tables and chairs. We sat down and discussed the price with the owner as well as what food she could offer. We agreed on ten different dishes to feed approximately sixty people, a waiter, tables and a stereo. We would have to decorate and supply the liquor which was on the long list that we had already made. We set our wedding date for the 20th of April, 2005.

We had two months to prepare and send out the invitations.
A friend I worked with agreed to make the invitations on his computer and print them off for me. One of my girlfriends volunteered to make name labels for the tables and one of Juan's friends wanted to decorate. The most stressful part for me was finding a dress.
I went to every store in Puerto Plata looking for *the one* but I couldn't find anything that I remotely liked at all. When I was almost ready to give up and tell Juan that we would have to get the bus to the next city in order to look for one, we came across a small shop in the middle of nowhere at the edge of the city. I tried not to get my hopes up as we parked Juan's scooter and walked up to the door.
I was pleasantly surprised when the shop owner welcomed us and told me that she bought all of her dresses in New York from David's Bridal Shop. She explained to me that she didn't sell the dresses; she only rented them. That was perfect for me!
I was extremely relieved when I came across one that I really liked within the first five minutes. It was a bright, silky, white strapless, with pearl beads all around the torso.
I tried it on and twirled around for Juan, it fit me perfectly. Our wedding was going to be perfect, or so I thought.

My mother told me there were eight of them coming for our wedding: my parents, my sister, my aunt and uncle, a cousin and two friends of the family.
I told her to ask my sister and cousin to be my bride's maids and to get blue dresses, my favorite color.
I had no idea what a *real* traditional wedding was supposed to be like but I used all the knowledge I had gathered from TV and the few weddings I had attended in my lifetime. I never asked anyone for advice. It was going to be exactly as we wanted, traditional or not.

The big day was approaching quickly and one Friday night we were relaxing in our small apartment lying in bed. The power was out as usual, so we decided to go to bed early.
"I love you Allison." Juan hugged me.
"I love you too baby." I kissed him. "Fiancé" I added and kissed him again.
He propped himself up on one arm so he could look down at me and he gazed into my eyes for a few peaceful seconds.
"You know that I love you more than anything in the whole world?" He paused. "I'm sorry for all the times I have hurt your feelings. I will try harder in the future to be a better man. I know I'm slack with the house chores but if you can please understand my roots I will try to understand yours." He paused to kiss me.
I could feel something special coming on so I laid there and delightedly listened to him pour his heart out to me.
"You are the best thing that has ever happened to me and I don't know what I would do without you. I want you to be my wife. Will you marry

me?" His gentle brown eyes looked down upon me, patiently waiting for my response.

"Yes." I giggled and pulled him closer snuggling up to his neck.

It was everything I had wanted him to say, it was perfect. I felt extremely confident about our relationship and as we made love and climaxed together, I hoped we would stay this happy forever.

Juan had to make most of the arrangements for the wedding because if I tagged along we would have had to pay more. While he was busy with that, I was trying to fill out the thick pile of paperwork my mother had received from a lawyer.

I needed Juan's whole life story. Every address he had ever lived at, every school he ever attended, information about his immediate family, their names, birthdays, and every detail possible about how we met. Our first kiss, our first present to each other, and it went on... Juan had moved around a lot as a child so it was very hard to find all the dates and addresses.

After I finally got the application filled out which took me a couple of weeks, we had to get his two birth certificates; yes there are two. We had to hire a certified translator to translate his records into English, and go to Santo Domingo to get his passport, medical exam and police report.

I quit my job two weeks before the wedding. I told my boss that I would be getting married and moving back to Canada soon afterwards. We were kind of lucky because the resort Juan worked at was closing for renovations and he received a small severance package when he was let go.

It was unfortunate that he lost his job but I was thrilled that he was able to spend the rest of my time there solely with me as well as a week with my family, which ended up being priceless.

My family was scheduled to arrive on April 16th, Saturday and the wedding was on the 20th a Wednesday.

It was raining the day they flew in.

Juan and I walked down the sidewalk wearing garbage bags as rain jackets towards the resort they were staying at to welcome them.

Their transfer bus tooted its horn as it passed.

Juan and I huddled under a small umbrella together trying not to get any wetter. My sister and cousin waved hysterically from the window at the back of the bus and I laughed as I waved back trying to control my excitement.

We met them in the lobby for a group hug. I was so happy that my family embraced my decision to marry this man and my mother and I had become civil towards each other again, my two biggest dilemmas solved.

We sat in the lobby for a while after they all had checked in and talked about the upcoming events.

"We want to pay for two nights on the resort for the both of you as a

wedding present." My Uncle hugged me.
"And we will pay for another night." My father smiled.
"Really, that would be awesome!" I jumped up and down.
I never expected that! I would get to spend even more time with them and have hot water! They didn't understand how much of a present this was going to be for us.
"We'll check in the day before the wedding and get ready here, and then honeymoon with you guys!" I smiled at my mother.
We eventually said goodbye and let them go to their rooms but made plans to meet the next day in the lobby around noon.

We woke up early the next morning and went to visit Juan's mother to tell her that my family had arrived before we took a moto concho to the resort complex.
My family met us in the lobby and followed us to the main road where we flagged down a guagua.
We were delivered right outside of my apartment shortly afterwards.
It was overcast and the air smelled like sweet, damp flowers and the ocean. Everyone was happy to finally see where I had been living all this time but they were also slightly horrified to see how small it was and the conditions I had to work with.
"There is a line of tiny bugs making a tunnel out of sand on your wall." My mother brought to my attention.
"Yeah mom, I know. I wipe it up every other day but they just keep on building it. Whatever." I laughed.
It was a huge culture shock for them to see how I lived.
I quickly wiped the astonishment off their faces and assured them that I had everything I needed and not to fuss, I was happy and was being well taken care of.

After they got their fill of my accommodation, which didn't take long, we took a taxi around the city and then went to the bottom of mount Isabella to go up in the cable car.
They were excited to go to the top and had been looking forward to it. I thought it was something touristy and fun that we could all do together.
Our group waited in line and then finally got ushered into a small cart that could fit about twenty people. All together, there were around sixteen of us inside and we had little room to move around.
I had been up the cable car twice before so I wasn't nervous but as we started getting higher and higher, everyone got tense.

When we were more than half way up, we could see the entire city and port. It was beautiful.
All of a sudden the cable car we were in shook forcefully and caught everyone off balance. We were two thousand feet in the air just 600 feet shy of the top.
My dad gracelessly fell on the floor and started rolling around trying to regain his balance in order to get up.
My heart almost stopped and I hugged Juan as hard as I could. My

sister started to cry and I thought to myself, if we die at least I will die with Juan by my side.

I looked at the man and girl who were operating the cable car and to my surprise they were hunched over, laughing hysterically which made me feel a little bit better. If they could laugh at a time like this, we might be okay.

I asked them in Spanish what was going on.

"Se fue la luz." The girl managed to roar.

"Oh my god" I said out loud. "The power went out guys." I told the cart full of terrified people.

An older lady who was standing next to my sister, who was sobbing, terrified for her life, tried to comfort her. "Oh dear, I can see why you are so scared you have your whole life ahead of you. Me, I'm old and have lived my life, but I think it's going to be okay."

We all laughed nervously at her comment which eased the tension as the cart stopped swaying and came to a complete stop.

We were hanging over a jungle of trees and rocks that were two thousand feet below us. I felt really bad for my family, I was naïve to the fact that the power went out all the time and I had never considered it happening while on the cable car.

I apologized and tried to comfort them by saying this must happen all the time.

"They change the cable every year." Juan announced to help calm everyone down. "We will be just fine."

We hung in the air for a few more minutes and then slowly started climbing the mountain again when the power came back on.

Still in a fright, we all held onto the railings, not wanting to lose our balance.

We disappeared into the clouds that surrounded the top of the mountain and right before we got to the top I felt another halt and we started swinging in the air again.

This time we were maybe 2500 feet above the city. My father tumbled to the floor again and started rolling around. He had a green book bag on his back that carried our water bottles and he had a few drinks into him already. We laugh now when we recall this terrifying memory when my dad looked like a ninja turtle rolling around on the floor and we all thought we were going to die.

We all ordered a large beer when we finally touched ground. I don't think anyone was looking forward to going back down anytime soon. We explored the shops and spent as much time as possible walking around; taking pictures and drinking beer hoping the way down would be a breeze.

Thank goodness the power stayed on for the descent. Everyone swore that they would never go on that cable car ever again. We went shopping for the rest of the day and safely returned my family back to the resort before supper. It was a very eventful day to say the least.

On Monday afternoon, Juan and I drove around the city confirming the flowers and the cake. We had to buy some last minute decorations and we also went to the place where I was renting my dress just to check in and make sure everything was still on track.

When we got there, the door was locked and there was a sign taped up that said "Gone to New York. Be back April 23rd."

"What are we going to do?" I cried as I banged on the door. "She left without telling us! Where am I supposed to get a dress now?"

No one came to the door and I sat down on the sidewalk trying to calm myself, but I was freaking out. I was getting married in two days.

"This would never happen in Canada" I cursed under my breath.

We argued as we drove around Puerto Plata to the same wedding shops again. I couldn't find anything.

"Another consequence of living the Dominican" I thought to myself. Everything is so laid back here that she probably forgot about renting the dress to me. We would have to go to Santiago by bus the next day in hope of finding something. If not, my wedding would be ruined.

We went to bed early that night so we could wake up in time for the bus but I couldn't sleep.

If I couldn't find a dress, what would I get married in? I couldn't believe this was really happening to me.

I cried in frustration as I brushed my teeth and got ready for bed.

"We will find you a dress Allison, don't worry. Stop crying, Okay?" Juan hugged me but I wasn't so sure.

8. Better Late than Never

We woke up the next morning at 7am and got ready to catch the early bus to Santiago.

"I'll be right back." Juan grabbed his keys. "I want to pass by again to see if she's there before we go to the station." Juan left as I finished making breakfast.

I was not very hopeful and was dreading the very long day ahead of us. We should have been at the resort with my family and not on a bus all day.

Juan appeared ten minutes later and poked his head in the doorway. To my surprise, he had a huge smile on his face.

"She's back!" He jumped towards me wrapping his arms tightly around my waist and picked me up. "I knocked on the door and woke her up. She arrived last night." He kissed me.

"Really?" I said in disbelief. "Let's go right now!" I needed to see for myself.

We ate breakfast and started packing a suitcase to give the lady some time to get up and then drove over.

Sure enough she was there and confirmed that she would have the dress ready for me.

I told her about the sign on her door and how I thought she had forgotten about me.

"I told one of my nephews to write that sign for me. He must have put the wrong date on it." She said casually.

"*Oh, the Dominican*" I said out loud as we left the store.

We asked Juan's aunt to drive us to the resort because we couldn't fit our bags on his scooter. I was so relieved that we didn't have to search for another dress all day.

We arrived at 2pm for check in and my mother met us in the lobby.

"This is my daughter Allison." My mother said as she introduced me to two pretty girls I'd never seen before. They were about my age and were wearing colourful bikinis under cover-ups that were mandatory in the lobby.

"You're the one who's marrying a Dominican?" One of them asked me.

"Yes! Tomorrow" I blushed.

"Oh my God, that is so awesome!" She squealed. "Your mother told me about your story and I think it is so cool. Is this him?" She held out her hand to Juan.

"Nice to meet you" Juan shook her hand.

"Congratulations!" She smiled, "Nice to meet both of you. Maybe we will see you later." They waved and walked towards the pool.

As we waited for the front desk agent to come over to assist us, I turned to my mother. "It is going to be so nice getting ready for the wedding with hot water and power. You have no idea!"

"Ah sweetie, I want to help you get ready." She smiled.

After Juan and I finally had our room keys, we left my mother behind and were escorted to our honeymoon suite.

As we unpacked our bags, I wandered around and was delighted to see that we had a living room and a kitchenette, I was just happy to have hot water. "Look Juan, we have a fridge and everything!" I danced around the room.

That night we stayed up later than we probably should have partying in my parent's large two bedroom suite.

I realized after a few minutes in their room that the hotel must have upgraded all of us because they found out on the day my parents arrived that I was getting married.

My family got to know Juan better as we played guitar and all sang along until 2am when we forced ourselves to go to bed.

I was very content as Juan and I walked back to our room holding hands and stealing kisses.

"What do you think of my family?" I asked.

"They're great! I had a lot of fun."

"That's good to hear, so in the future when you find out how crazy we all are, I hope you will remember your opinion from tonight." I looked at him seriously.

Our wedding day finally came! Juan woke up early and went into the city to rent a car while I stayed in bed waiting for him to come back but shortly after he left, my phone rang and woke me up.

"Allison, you have to get a taxi here right now. We need a major credit card."

"Oh" I complained. I felt stupid because even though I had never rented a car before I knew we would need a credit card and with all the excitement going on I never thought about it.

"It will take me like a half an hour to get to the main road and get a moto concho." I whined.

"No you have to get a taxi. I have to pick up the flowers in thirty minutes."

"Okay."

I dragged myself to the lobby where I tried to barter in Spanish for a lower price with the taxi drivers there but I quickly gave up when the guy just wouldn't believe that I lived there even though I was speaking Spanish.

He wouldn't go any lower in price than 500 Pesos to the boulevard which was only 10 minutes away by car. I could have gone to the main road and paid thirty Pesos for a moto. I was so annoyed.

When we had everything sorted out and I rented the car with my Visa, the first stop was to pick up the flowers and then back to the resort for my sister and cousin.

We then got dropped off to have our hair done at this small place out of someone's house that Juan's sister had recommended. We arrived around 11am and it took four hours to do our hair. I had to translate the whole time as best as I could as we took turns having our heads covered in rollers and hairspray before we sat under the dreadful hot hair dryers. I called Juan around 3pm when we were ready to leave and asked to get picked up as soon as possible.

Half an hour later when our ride finally arrived, it started to rain. My bridesmaids were getting cranky; neither of them had eaten anything all day and the rain was threatening our perfectly curled hair. We had to stop at the restaurant first before we went back to the resort to get something to eat which they were not too happy about either.

"I'm so hungry" my sister reminded me.

"I know me too but we have to stop for just one second I promise."

We got out of the car and rushed up to the restaurant trying to cover our hair with our purses. When we were safely under the roof I was surprised to see the decorations were almost done. The name tags were on the tables and there were balloons tied up everywhere. Juan and his friend Felix had done all the decorating and I was extremely impressed.

"This is amazing!" My mouth dropped.

It was better than I'd expected. Each table was dressed with a white and light baby blue table cloth and flower centerpieces positioned perfectly. The flower guy had to dye the flowers blue for me because he didn't have any blue flowers and that was the colour I had to have. The cake was the only thing that was missing and that was the last thing we had to get picked up.

When we arrived back at the resort we all rushed to the snack bar and finally ate lunch. The clock was ticking and after I tore into a salad to ensure I would fit into my dress, Juan and I rushed to our room so I could start my makeup and help him with his suit.

"Did you ever hear of the tradition that you aren't allowed to see the bride on the wedding day before you get married?" I giggled as I slapped his bum.

"Really?" he grabbed my waist, pulled me close and kissed me. "I guess we didn't follow that tradition."

"Are you nervous?" I looked into his gentle brown eyes.

"Not one bit. I can't wait to be able to call you my wife." He smiled.

"Are you nervous?" He asked me.

"No." I laughed as there was a knock at the door and my mother came rushing in. "What can I do?" She asked.

When we were beautified we walked to the lobby to wait for our driver, a friend of Juan's family who volunteered.

I wore a pretty sundress and Juan carried the heavy wedding dress for me.

My parents showed up shortly afterward and the first car load of us left the resort around 5:30pm.

Our photographer was waiting at the restaurant and after I changed into my wedding dress he took us in his vehicle to the beach for some

pictures.
Luckily, it stopped raining just long enough to get a few good shots and then we returned to the restaurant and joined the party of guests that had arrived. That was when it started pouring down rain.

My mother had brought bubbles, pretty little bags of chocolate kisses and confetti that she distributed to all the tables. The bubbles turned out to be a big hit, everyone loved them.
I was glowing with joy looking around at all of my family and friends. The decorations were perfect, the cake was huge and I tried hard to talk to everyone there which was almost impossible.

As the clock struck 6:45pm Juan's mother still hadn't arrived and I started to worry. I found Juan, who was having a great time with his friends, drinking the Champaign cider we had bought and posing for group pictures with his fellow animation coworkers, I was definitely more worried than he was.
"Don't worry, she will be here." Juan smiled.
At 7:30pm Juan's mother finally arrived but the judge still hadn't showed up and we planned on saying "I Do" at 7pm sharp or at least that is what was stated on the invitations.
"Oh, the Dominican" I said under my breath for the hundredth time.
"Juan" I yelled for him to come over to me. "Where is the judge? What if she forgets? This is crazy!" I panicked.
"Remember baby, we are in the Dominican. She will be here soon." He patted me on the shoulder and rejoined his friends.
I sat down at my family's table and tried to stay calm. I looked around and noticed that no one else seemed worried. Juan's friends were entertaining us even though they had no intention of doing so, a few regulars from Juan's resort who wanted to come were there socializing with everyone. All our friends and most of Juan's family were all laughing, blowing bubbles, and drinking as much free liquor as they could. I slowly started to calm down.
"She will be here soon." I smiled at my father who had sensed my anxiety.

My family couldn't speak a lick of Spanish so they stayed together at the one table they were assigned to.
Juan and I brought his immediate family over and introduced them for the first time.
They smiled and hugged timidly as Juan and I translated for them.
It was slightly awkward. When two people get married their families usually know each other and are at least able to converse with each other, but not in our case.

The judge finally showed up at 8pm and apologized for being late, the wedding she was coming from went later than she thought it would. We quickly rushed into our positions.
Regrettably, I forgot my bouquet when my father and I hurried around the corner to wait for the song "Here Comes The Bride" to start.

On our cue my father and I slowly walked around the corner and down the aisle I had created towards my husband to be. Everyone stood respectfully and admired me with big smiles as I admired Juan, waiting for me at the other end of the terrace.
"I love ya sweetie" my father whispered to me as he let go of my arm.
I joined Juan, my two bridesmaids and his groomsmen behind the table that faced everyone.
The judge went on for what seemed to be forever in Spanish and I couldn't really understand very much of what she was saying other than when it was my turn to say "I do."
I stood there in disbelief that I was twenty years old and getting married. I just couldn't believe that it was finally happening after everything we had been through and all the time that had passed. I crossed my fingers, hoping that our marriage would last forever.

After we signed all of the legal documents, which took forever, everyone formed a line to congratulate me with a hug and a kiss. It must have been a Dominican custom because I was not expecting it but in the end I was pleased that I got to kiss everyone that came to see me get married, even the people I didn't know.
My parents merged close to the front of the line "Now you are his responsibility" my dad giggled and hugged me.

The food was uncovered and we lined up to serve ourselves from the buffet.
The photographer filmed Juan and I as we fed each other a bottle of expensive Champaign that we'd bought for with our supper and when we finished eating the photographer got everyone prepared for some group pictures.

After a very professional photo shoot, my father and uncle brought their guitars out to play our wedding song and my sister got ready to sing with them.
"We will stand here... we should move this table back" I directed when all of the sudden everything went dark. I looked around mystified.
"Oh no" I moaned. "The power is out."
I tried to look at the positive side of things. This will be another crazy story to tell.
Thankfully, an emergency light came on and my uncle played a bit of guitar to pass the time as we waited for the power to come back on.
"Just my luck" I thought as I sat down with a glass of wine, hoping it wouldn't last for too long.
"Can you take me to the bathroom?" My sister came over to me with a silly grin on her face.
"This way sissy" I motioned for her to follow me.
"How long do you think the lights will be out?" She laughed.
"You never know" I complained as I made my way through the darkness and into the bathroom.
"Oh my God!" My sister screamed. "What was that?" she pointed to

the floor and backed up.
"What?" I said as I calmly looked around.
It was so dark inside the restroom that I could barely see the floor. I had a lighter and started flicking it.
A cockroach scampered across the floor about an inch from our open toe shoes.
"AAAHHH" My sister screamed and jumped out of the bathroom. "It's a cockroach isn't it?" she shrieked.
"It's gone." I said calmly as I looked around. They never stay out in the open for more than a few seconds.
"You can use the bathroom now." I flicked my lighter a few more times so she could see that it was gone.
She gave me a nervous look, hesitated and carefully tip-toed into the bathroom stall, leaving the door ajar.
That was her first cockroach encounter. If she only knew they could fly, I shuttered.

Forty five minutes later the lights came back on and we finally had our first dance. It was perfect and I couldn't stop smiling at the video camera.
Everyone cheered for us and then the camera man directed us over to the cake where Juan held my hand as I cut the first piece.
Juan's aunt came over and stood next to us and took over the job of serving which I was thankful for, I think we had a ten pound cake, it was massive.
The photographer came to my side and told me it was time to throw my bouquet.
We gathered all the single ladies. It was a pathetic throw on my part, I didn't even throw it far enough to reach the group of girls; they had to jump forward to grab it. Juan's cousin was the lucky girl who jumped for it first and as we got our picture taken together the guy taking the video placed a chair in the middle of the open space, stood back and cleared his throat.
"Okay, vamanos!" He sat me down into the chair and told Juan to "preparense".
Juan knew what he had to do and stuck his head under my dress.
His mother stood up in shock. The bewildered look on her face made me burst out laughing and she slowly sat back down.
It took Juan a few minutes while he struggled to keep his hands behind his back but he finally got the garter belt off my leg and gathered the single men.
Juan threw it behind his back and mostly everyone jumped out of the way.
"Ah" I thought to myself, "they want to continue playing the field, typical."

At 11pm I changed back into in to my sun dress and was excited to start partying. I eagerly looked for Juan and when I found him I noticed

that he was handing out the gallons of rum we had bought for the party.
"What are you doing, baby?" I ran over.
"I'm so tired."
"But this is our wedding! We're supposed to stay up late and party." I grabbed the bottle of rum out of his hand.
"We can party on the resort." He smiled. "My family doesn't drink and they are ready to go home."
He thanked the people who started to leave and we waited for our driver to take us back to the resort, I was disappointed but he was right.

We made a grand entrance into the lobby carrying flowers and wedding cake and the few people who were there clapped and cheered as we passed them on our way to the bar for a celebration drink.
"Cheers!" My father raised his glass.
"Salud!" I cheered.
"It was a beautiful wedding Allison." My aunt tapped her cup with mine.
"Thanks for coming everyone. It wouldn't have been the same without all of you here." I was so grateful that they came and that they all liked Juan, which made me so happy.
We had a few drinks and talked about my plan to move back home in a few weeks and we shared in Juan's excitement that he would be coming to Canada hopefully within a year.
"So husband…" I grabbed his hand. "Shall we go to bed?"

We were exhausted but as soon as we shut the door to our room Juan started the shower.
"Care to join me?" He dropped his pants. "The water is warm."
He grabbed me and unzipped my dress. He knocked my straps aside and swiftly undid my bra.
He caressed my breasts as he led me into the shower and under the warm water that I had always taken for granted. Needless to say our marriage was consummated.

I woke up early the next morning to the gentle hum of the cool crisp air in our room and the sunshine pouring in through the curtains. I propped myself up over my husband and kissed him gently. I embraced every second as I watched him slowly wake up.
"I had a great time last night." I smiled.
"Shall we go for breakfast my wife?" He tickled me softly and I squirmed away out of bed.
I turned on the hot water in the shower. "Care to join me husband?" I slipped my shirt over my head. "Breakfast can wait for us."

After we ate, we decided to go see Juan's mother as well as the photographer and the camera guy to get our pictures and wedding video.
Surprisingly my mother wanted to come with us. We thought it was a great idea and the three of us walked to the main road and flagged down two moto conchos.

Juan jumped on the first one and told the second driver to follow him as I instructed my mother to get on the motorcycle first and I would sit behind her.

She held on tightly as our driver manoeuvred his way through the busy traffic.

We paid the drivers and walked a few minutes up a long dirt road lined with small colourful houses, tightly fitted together with very little space in between each building. Juan's mother's apartment was near the end of the road.

Everyone stared at us as we walked by. Small children stopped playing and curiously watched until we passed.

"Watch out!" Juan yelled as he jumped in front of my mother and pushed us into someone's open front door. Juan rushed in behind us as I saw a very startled young woman sitting in a chair right in front of us with her eyes wide open. She was no doubt surprised to see two white girls hurry into her house uninvited.

Juan said something to her in Spanish which made her facial expression go calm and she smiled.

"There is a man out there with a gun." Juan anxiously explained while peeking outside of the door. "I think he is drunk. You don't know what he might do, especially with the two of you here." He pointed at me.

I was nervous and I could only imagine how my inexperienced mother felt.

We hid in the stranger's house until Juan said it was okay to leave. The man with the gun had left and stumbled further down the street.

We thanked the woman who was watching us from her chair and we hurried to Juan's mother's house where she quickly offered us beans and rice and kissed each of our cheeks.

We spent a couple of hours with his family eating and relaxing by the open door. My mother sat in the corner observing, not understanding anything that was being said just like I had done in the past. I think she was slightly relieved when we left to go see the wedding pictures and pick up our video.

The photographer had done a very good job. He showed us the pictures and we chose a certain number of them to be printed.

We paid him and returned back to the resort before supper.

We found the rest of our group at the bar and enthusiastically joined them.

"So mom, do you want to tell everyone about your day?" I smiled sarcastically at her.

Even though the weather was poor the entire time my family was there, we made the best of it. My sister, our father and I even got on stage one night for karaoke where we received a standing ovation afterwards for singing the song "Country Roads".

We were sad to check out when the end of our honeymoon finally came and even sadder to see my family leave.

"I will come home soon, probably in a few weeks." I hugged my father. "Have a safe trip back and I'll see you soon."

With all the wedding excitement over, Juan and I had to get back on track with all the immigration paperwork, translating everything into English and whatever else my lawyer told me to do through email. We went to Santo Domingo for a day and got his medical exam done and criminal record check papers from the police.

We had many pictures to send in with our application that were extremely helpful. We looked so young when we first met and in our wedding pictures you could see that a lot of time had passed.

I found out that in order to sponsor someone you need to meet certain financial requirements to ensure you are able to support the applicant. The sponsor is also legally responsible for the applicant for three years after they land which meant for example, if the applicant leaves the sponsor for whatever reason and goes on social assistance, welfare or whatever the case, the sponsor is required by law to pay for that assistance as part of the contract they signed with the government. That made me nervous because there are no guarantees when you sponsor someone but I was hopeful that we wouldn't end up being a statistic.

Two weeks after we married I had finished gathering all of the information required for Juan's application and had to mail it to the Canadian Embassy in Ottawa, and find a job as soon as possible so I would be able to meet the financial requirements and support the both of us when Juan eventually came to live with me.

I booked a flight from Santiago, connecting in Newark and then to Canada. It was cheaper to fly from there compared to Puerto Plata even with the bus and cab fare included.

The day I had to leave was a very sad one. After living with Juan for nine months and sharing our lives together, I was devastated to have to return back to our phone relationship but it was for a bigger purpose and I had no choice.

Juan came with me on the Caribe Tours bus to Santiago to see me off. I held back my tears the whole way while I held his hand tightly. I kept looking at him, trying to remember every little detail about his hands, his face, his lips. I had no idea when I was going to see him again.

When we arrived, he took my bags and helped me flag down a cab that would take me to the airport.

When a cab stopped in front of us, tears started falling down my cheeks as Juan bargained with the driver, this was really happening.

He turned to me and saw that I was falling apart and hugged me tightly. My heart ached as he kissed me deeply and told me it was going to be okay.

"We will be together soon, I love you." He reassured me.

I forced myself through the motions of watching my suitcase go in the trunk and then getting into the back of the cab.

As I started driving away from him, I turned around in the backseat and watched him get smaller and smaller. I held back my tears until my throat hurt; this was the start of the hardest few months of my life.

My father picked me up at the airport when I landed and as he scooped me up in his strong arms I started to cry.

"It's going to be okay sweetie, I promise. Don't cry." He rocked me in his arms.

After a few minutes he released me, smiled sympathetically and took my suitcase. He carried it to the car as I followed with my head hung low. I was happy to be back nevertheless because I would have hot water and power and customer service. I would pay the same prices as everyone else and I wouldn't be the minority anymore which was a big relief, but I would have all those nice things without the man I loved.

Now I had to start a waiting game where I would have no control over anything.

"I wonder what my friends will think now." I thought as I felt a small comfort from the familiar dull scenery.

9. Waiting

I moved back in with my parents and mailed the application to sponsor Juan during the second week of May.

I found two jobs at two different restaurants; one as a cook and one as a waitress and I took both of them.

I worked six days a week (sometimes seven), and mostly twelve hour days all summer long. I missed Juan so desperately that unless I was extremely busy I couldn't keep my mind off him. It killed me inside not knowing when he would be approved for his Visa and we could be together again.

Time crawled by and it eventually got a bit easier after the first five months.

When September arrived I realized I would have to move to the city because the town I worked in was very seasonal, everything closed at the beginning of October.

My sister was starting college and my cousin also wanted to get an apartment, so we got a three bedroom place together in the city to save money.

I found a great job at a hotel and grew more impatient as I waited for a letter or anything to tell me the progress of Juan's application. The immigration website said "in process" every time I checked. I eventually gave up hoping that it would tell me something new.

My mother was enthusiastic about embracing my husband's culture. She found a website where people posted questions about Dominicans abroad and about immigration.

She posted where we lived and that her daughter just married Juan from Puerto Plata and she wanted to know if there were any other Dominicans in the same province.

There were a few responses congratulating her and a few Dominicans from the Atlantic Provinces said hi but no one confirmed that they lived in Halifax.

There was however another response from a girl asking about Juan. Her comment was something like this:

"*Congratulations on your daughter's marriage. Did she marry Juan Fransisco that used to work in Playa Dorada at 'this' hotel*?"

My mother confirmed yes, that was him and the girl went on to comment again:

"*Oh I'm so sorry. I was actually engaged to him a year ago and found out that he was cheating on me so I called it off, I'm pretty sure that we are talking about the same person. I'm sorry but I just wanted you to know who your daughter is getting herself mixed up with.*"

Of course my mother rushed to show me the startling comment from this strange unknown girl and after reading it I was quite disturbed. She had spelled his last name wrong and I knew she was lying because I had lived with him a year ago. I honestly thought it must have been the same girl who tried to assault me at the bar. I got on the computer in a rage and responded to her comment:

"I don't know who you are but I know you're lying, you spelled his last name wrong. This is Juan's wife and I can't believe you would try to upset my mother like this, if you have some solid proof, I would like to see it."

There were a few more unfriendly words back and forth but eventually I stopped going to that website and brushed it off as *crazy girl*. I did however tell Juan all about it.
"I think that must be either the same girl who tried to fight with you at the club or maybe it's one of her friends. She tried to get my fired at work a couple times when she found out that you were living with me. I am so sorry that she is saying things like this. I was never engaged to anyone else ever, I promise." He sounded sincere.
I was truly surprised that I had to tolerate women saying these types of things to me. I never imagined that random girls who may have had some sort of relationship with my husband in the past would try to harass me after we were married and expect to break us up. All I could do was try to ignore these comments and threats, and keep believing that they were lies, what else was I going to do?

My father passed away at the end of September of 2005, five months after I got married. He had been taken to the hospital again but this time he was too sick to recover. It was especially difficult for me to deal with because I had moved out of his house when I was a teenager, moved away for college a year later and then moved even farther away to the Caribbean. I had missed so much time with him. I felt even worse that I wasn't aware of just how serious his situation was. My father had always been my rock; he meant more to me than he knew and wished I could have told him that.
Juan and I used to talk about how my father would teach him all kinds of man things when he finally arrived. We were looking forward to so many things that would never happen.
On top of the pain from being away from my husband and not knowing what he was doing, where he was or when I would see him again, I had to accept the death of my father at the young age of forty-five.

I started drinking a lot more to mask my pain and I became even more depressed. I comforted myself with food but that turned out to be even worse than the alcohol when I started gaining weight.
I looked to Juan for support but there was only so much he could do

with the distance between us. His new job as an animator at a resort outside of Puerto Plata had more of a party atmosphere that kept him busy. He was given a room right outside the resort so he wouldn't have to travel at all and I could tell from our many phone conversations that he too was partying a lot more but for different reasons. He was staying up all night with tourists and friends; I prayed he was being faithful. It became unbearable to even think of my own husband. I wouldn't come out and bluntly ask him if he was cheating because he would definitely say no. My suspicions and accusations caused by fear, grief and helplessness caused many arguments between us. We were growing apart.

On December 22nd Juan called me with good news.

"Guess what baby! The letter…" Juan cheered through the phone. "I got the letter today from the embassy!"

"What does it say? Can you come soon?" I was so relieved; I wasn't sure how much longer our relationship could withstand the distance.

"It says that I have to go to Santo Domingo and drop off my passport so they can put the Visa inside, and they will call me when it's ready."

We were both overjoyed with the thought that we would see each other soon. However it didn't say exactly how long it would take before they would call. I hated not even knowing an estimated time frame.

He took the bus to Santo Domingo the next day and dropped his passport off at the embassy and then returned home to wait.

We were lucky they hadn't requested an interview with him, which would have meant another trip to the capital for Juan and more time waiting. They would have asked him various questions about our relationship with dates as well as my personal information like my address, birthday, and phone number, my family's names and his intentions. Many applicants had to be interviewed but I think because we had been together for over three years and the pictures I had sent visually proved that a lot of time had passed, I believe that helped convince them that our relationship was genuine as well as my wedding pictures with both of our families together.

Two weeks later we still hadn't heard anything and I was getting more and more miserable every day.

"Maybe you should call them." I complained through the phone.

"That won't do anything. We just have to wait. They should call me soon. Can't you go online and check the status of my application?" Juan asked.

"I did. It doesn't say anything. They should have let you know when to expect the call."

"I know, but they didn't." Juan raised his voice. "I'm just as frustrated as you. I want to be with you more than anything but how do you think I feel? I have to leave my family, my job and all my friends. I want to get the call right now too but having you yell at me is making things worse."

I sighed, "I'm sorry. It's just not fair. I miss you so much."

As time painfully went on, my mother continued searching blogs and websites for other women who had also married Dominicans. She ended up meeting a nice woman on a popular blog and after they chatted online for a few days she gave the woman my phone number. This girl called me one evening breaking my schedule of feeling lonely and sorry for myself as usual. Her call was like a breath of fresh air. She lived in Ontario and had been married to a Dominican for a couple of years and they had a child. She told me the story of how she met her husband and explained how long her immigration application took from the time she submitted it to the time her husband arrived.

She also answered all of my questions about the process and the steps that are required after you submit the application.

I told her my story and whined about how hard it was to not know what was going to happen or when. She comforted me by relating to exactly what I was going through.

We spent close to an hour on the phone talking about the good and bad and how hard it is to adjust to life in a new country. She also gave me very valuable information that I would never have discovered on my own anytime soon.

One thing she said that I never forgot was "When you are married to a Dominican you are married to his whole family. When he moves here, everyone in his family will want money. His third cousin replaced and a step brother half removed will want help."

I didn't realize at that time how true this was and how I would have to learn how to accept this into our budget and not think of it as an extra expense.

When I hung up the phone I felt so much better, I wasn't as alone as I had believed.

January 16th 2006, eight months after I submitted Juan's application and almost a month after he dropped off his passport, he called me early in the morning and woke me up.

"They called me! I'll take the bus to Santo Domingo tomorrow morning and get my Visa!" He was thrilled.

"Okay, okay," I stuttered, "I will start looking for flights. When can you leave?" I fell out of bed.

"Whenever you can get me a flight I guess. Are you okay? What was that noise?"

"Nothing" I composed myself. "I'm so excited. I can't believe it is finally happening!"

"I will quit my job tomorrow afternoon. My boss is going to freak out." He had many ties to cut and loved ones to say goodbye to in a very short period of time. I felt bad for him.

Juan caught the bus the following day at 5:00am. He had to wait in a long line up at the embassy.

When he finally made it to the counter and was handed his passport, he

quickly found a quiet spot to sit down.
He opened his passport and looked inside making sure his Visa was there. He smiled as he studied it and sighed. He was finally allowed to leave the country.
He left the embassy with his head held high.

During the long four hour ride back home he was nervous and excited as he thought about telling his boss that this was his last shift, he wondered if he had enough time to say goodbye to all of his family and his excitement conquered his fear as he thought about his future.

I spent my entire day online and then went to travel agencies searching for a flight to bring him to me. I couldn't find anything available until five days later or more, I couldn't accept that.
"Juan the soonest flight I can find is in five days. I can't wait that long." I complained.
"I will look here too." He said. "I might be able to get flights from here that you can't get from there."
He drove from travel agent to travel agent as well hoping to find something.
The hardest part was he couldn't fly into the United States because his Visa was valid for travel to Canada only so that really limited our options for airlines. He had to fly direct.

He called me a couple of hours later and told me very happy news! He found a flight leaving in three days on the 21st of January.
I cringed when he told me that he would need thirty-seven thousand Pesos to pay for it. That was approximately $1300 Canadian and it was pretty much all the savings I had. I was troubled that I would have to spend all of it on a one way flight however I didn't hesitate as I withdrew it from my account and walked to western union to send it to him.
"I don't care how much it costs." I huffed and puffed over the phone. It was freezing outside and I was waiting for the bus. "I want to see you now so you better quit your job and say goodbye to your family ASAP." I shivered. "Call me back after you buy the ticket so I know what time you arrive."

Juan quit his job that night, surprising the heck out of his boss. He kept it a secret that he was waiting for a Visa. The resort might not have hired him if they knew he would be leaving a few months later. He was a good employee and they didn't want to let him go.

After a very emotional two days of saying goodbye to his family and friends, he was scheduled to fly out of Puerto Plata in the morning to connect in Montreal for an arrival of 11pm into my arms.
My mother, sister and one of my good friends all came to the airport with me and as we drove there, I couldn't stop worrying about my husband. It was his first time flying and he had to take two planes.
"I hope he doesn't have turbulence. I can see him now in the Montreal airport all alone and confused, I hope he's okay." I worried out loud to

my entourage.
On top of all that, I was so nervous to see him. I couldn't believe I had waited for this moment for nine months and it was right around the corner and I felt sick to my stomach. I tried to stay calm as we all anticipated his arrival.

At 11:30pm we were still waiting for his flight to arrive. We were getting restless so I went to check the status board.
"Oh no" I moaned. "His connecting flight from Montreal was cancelled and now he's connecting in Ottawa as well. He won't be here till 1am." I was so mad.
"I am so sorry guys." I whined as I slouched back down on the floor.

It seemed like forever as we tried to stay awake waiting outside the domestic arrivals. I wondered if Juan would look any different from the last time I had seen him. What would he have for luggage and would he be happy with his new home? Would it be different between us because of the time that had passed? I was so stressed and I should've been jumping for joy.
"Look!" My mother pointed to some people starting to come out from the arrivals door.
We all stood up as Juan walked through the door and I snapped a picture of him.
He did look different. He wore a leather jacket that I later learned his friend gave him saying that it was the warmest jacket he owned. He carried a small black duffel bag and he looked just as stressed as I felt.
We kissed briefly and I introduced him to my friend for the first time.
It was an exciting drive back to the apartment as Juan told us about his first snow ball in Montreal, his first Canadian beer in Ottawa and how nervous he was going through immigration with his Visa.

We had a few friends and family waiting for us at our apartment and surprisingly when we got back they were still awake waiting for us.
I sat on Juan's lap as we all listened to the story of his travels.
At 2:30am I told everyone we were going to bed and led Juan by the hand up to his new room where I tore his clothes off.

I had taken two days off from work to spend with him while he was going through *his* culture shock.
I started to realize how lucky we both were that I had the chance to live in his country for a while before he came to mine. He had seen me through my culture shock and now I could see him through his, but with experience.
I was more understanding towards many things he did that weren't acceptable in his new home because I knew why he did them.
He would always leave the door open when he entered a residence and he never took his shoes off until someone asked him to, just like he was used to in his country. He was extremely picky with the new food he was presented with and he was unfamiliar and a little destructive with some of the appliances we had because he had never used them before.

He was, on the other hand, quite happy with how organized the traffic was compared to his city and how clean the streets were, but it was freezing and life moves at such a quicker pace than he was used to. He tried very hard to be punctual.

My mother stayed at our apartment for a couple days to drive us around. We had to go shopping for winter clothes, summer clothes and everything in between.

At the end of the day when we returned home, I asked Juan to model his new outfits for us.

We all laughed as he came around the corner bundled up in a huge winter coat, gloves, a hat and boots. He giggled and walked with his arms and legs stuck out, pretending that he was having a hard time moving.

"How do you live like this?" He laughed. "I never thought I would ever wear this many clothes at the same time." He started sweating and unzipped his coat.

An ironic thing was that my cousin who had played that prank on me with the nasty email in high school was living with us at the time and he quickly became good friends with Juan. When I was at work my cousin would take him out and show him how to use the bus system and help him distribute resumes. I was thankful but very protective of my husband because I had waited so long to have him with me in Canada. I was nervous that he would get lost somewhere or that people would be racist towards him or that he might be in the wrong place at the wrong time. I worried about him constantly.

It took three long boring cold months for Juan to find a job. It seemed like no one would hire him because he was an immigrant. His English was good but not perfect and his strong accent didn't help the situation.

Eventually, through a friend's good recommendation, we found him a job working in a warehouse driving a forklift. He was just happy to get out of the house and finally make some money. He came to realize that his new job was hard work compared to dancing around with tourists all day.

"Money really doesn't grow on trees here." He joked. "A lot of people think you go to Canada and the money is everywhere. It's harder to make money here than I thought."

"You have no idea, baby." I told him. "You are lucky that I am very thrifty!" He was soon to find out just how much.

As time passed, we had a hard go at keeping our relationship on track. We fought like all couples do but this time it was Juan who had nowhere to go and no one to turn to and in my opinion most Dominican men have bad tempers. I sympathized with him because I knew how it felt but that was just the way it was. Life isn't fair sometimes.

Juan and I lived with my sister and my cousin until the lease was up seven months after Juan arrived and then got our own place in

September. Our first place in Canada together!
It was an older two bedroom unit in a low income area so the price was great! The neighbours, not so much. Most of the people who lived in the building were on government support and not many of them worked, so they were always home making noise.
"Now we can do whatever we want!" I smiled at my husband as we stood in our new living room surrounded by boxes and furniture. "We should get a computer."
"Take it easy." Juan was overwhelmed with all the work we had in front of us to put our new apartment together. "We need to think about going back to see my family before we get a computer."
"Okay baby. We will do that first." I hugged him. "Don't worry. We'll go in a few months. I promise."
"Okay, break it up. There are more boxes in the car." My mother came in with her arms full.

We had a party when we were settled and invited all of our Latin friends. Our new place was anything but fancy but we were always looking for excuses to party.
"A new Dominican just arrived last week!" One of our friends advised the group of people in our small living room.
"Really! That is awesome! A new addition to our group!" I smiled. "He came through a marriage Visa?"
"Of course, probably" he laughed.
"That will bring us up to six Dominicans!" I cheered.

As the months passed I really wanted a computer, especially so Juan could use it to connect with his family and read the news from his home town. I was hoping that it would help with his homesickness so I saved up enough money and that Christmas, I bought a new desktop computer at a great price. I couldn't believe we had gone for that long without one.

One afternoon when I got home from work, I checked Juan's email as I did every so often for my own piece of mind, in hopes that he didn't have some other girlfriend somewhere. We both had each other's passwords to make it fair, but really it was stupid because he could have had another email that I didn't know about.
I signed in to his email and one of the subject lines caught my attention. It was from a girl and so I opened it.

"Juan you might not remember me but we slept together about a year and a half ago. Just the once however it was enough, I had your baby. I tried calling you at the hotel when I found out but it was closed. Thankfully, I found you on an online forum. I don't mean to cause you any trouble but you need to know. Deny me, but not your child. His name is John. I want nothing from you and hope you and your wife are happy. He is now 6 months old. If your wife reads this, please tell her that I mean no harm, I just thought it was right that you knew the truth,

Enjoy your life in Canada."

"That lying cow" I fumed. "If your wife reads this..." that is exactly what she wanted to happen.
I waited impatiently for Juan to get home from work so I could confront him. If it was true, that meant that he cheated on me with this girl. I was distraught but I told myself it was probably just another girl who was obsessed with Juan when he worked on the resorts. I should wait and give him a chance to check his email and see how he reacts before I say anything I thought to myself.

After he was home for a few hours and was using the computer, I went and stood over him.
"Did you check your email today?" I asked cunningly
"Yeah, why?" He responded, looking up from the monitor.
"I think you know why." I said harshly. "Is it true?"
"What do you mean? Did you check my email?"
"Yes" I stared him in the eyes.
"What do you think?" He paused "Of course it's not true." He defended himself.
"You should write her back." I impatiently sat down beside him and waited.
I could see his brain overloading on what he should do and after a few uncomfortable moments he clicked on reply.
I watched him as he typed his response telling the girl she had the wrong person; he didn't know her. He asked her to send a picture of herself and the baby if it was his.
I felt better but was still very suspicious and I couldn't stop thinking "What if Juan had a child out there? What if he had numerous children? What if this woman tried to come after him for child support?"

The girl responded the next day as I expected she would.
She attached a small picture of a child, side on from the chest up and said that she only wanted her child to know his father.
Juan looked hard at the picture. "I can't believe this." He said out loud. "He doesn't even look a thing like me. She could have tried to find a more convincing picture. This girl is trying to cause problems for us."
I was silent. I wanted to believe him, but a small part of me knew that in long distance relationships, married or not, things can happen. It wasn't like we hadn't had a crazy woman mad with jealousy try to break us up before. Maybe this was the same girl who tried to challenge me at the bar, or maybe all the things that were happening were caused by all different women. I had a small feeling inside telling me it was very possible that she could be telling the truth.
Juan wrote her back and said that he didn't believe her, and for her to send the picture that he asked for of herself or leave him alone.

The next day like clockwork she responded again and reassured him that she hoped that he was happy with his wife and she was only trying

to contact him in the best interest of the child. She was quite nice to him considering the circumstances but again she didn't send any more pictures.
"Juan can I have your permission to email her?" I asked firmly.
He agreed after some hesitation, maybe to get me off his back about checking his email every five minutes but also because he realized that I was very upset and might be silently questioning if he was being honest with me.
I responded from my own email address:

"*This is Juan's wife. I have been advised about what is going on and I am seeing things from both sides. I just wanted to let you know that Juan will never admit that he cheated on me. Can you somehow prove that it's his baby through DNA? How did you think he would react to this without any type of proof? Did you think we would come visit you in England and just believe that it's his child after a couple emails and a small picture that he can't even make out? Who are you trying to convince here? I am tired of girls who are obsessed with my husband and want to break us up. Are you the same girl who tried to tell me that he slept with someone who had no teeth? Until you can get serious about trying to prove this is his child, then leave us alone.*"

That was, of course, followed by a very nasty response from her. One part of what she said was:

"*Dear child, please stop being so naive... You have been made a fool of long enough, haven't you? You are young and thankfully after you split up, which you will, you will still be young enough to move on!
Good luck.*"

We sent another couple hostile emails back and forth. A girl loves a good cat fight, but it got old and she wasn't making any effort to prove anything, she was just verbally attacking me so I decided to end the fight and wrote her one last email.

"I want you to know that I am truly sorry that you'll have to raise a child as a single mother. That is something no parent should have to do alone. I hope you find a good man to help raise your child and if you are unwilling to prove what you are saying is true then please leave us alone and I wish you all the best in the future."

She didn't respond. I decided that from the small single picture she sent of a child, in absence of a picture of herself that Juan had requested and the insulting words insinuating that she actually knew of the both of us for a considerable amount of time, (you have been made a fool of long enough) she had to be lying. Juan and I agreed never to speak of it again; she was unwilling to prove it and it was too upsetting for me to think about. Even if the story had some truth to it or, I hate to say, even if it was all true, what was I supposed to do? I thought deep down that if this woman told Juan that she had his child, she would have been prepared to prove it to him and not expect him to believe it from an email, especially when she wouldn't send the picture of herself, the only thing that Juan had wanted. I couldn't believe it.

What would you have done? Some girls are crazy and when they have their eyes set on a man they'll do whatever it takes to win him over, especially when he worked on the animation staff and had to be overly friendly and accommodating to the ladies which led them on.

The first time we went on vacation to visit Juan's family was thirteen months after he landed in Canada. He was very homesick and missed his family more than anything. The winter made him depressed. Everyone's door was always closed, there was no place to go in the streets where you could just hang out and there was not a lot to do without having to pay for it.

I have a big family but I only associated with a handful of them on a regular basis and my husband couldn't understand that at all. "Family is everything." He would say.

We flew into Puerto Plata together on February 9th 2006. When the engines fired up and our heads were sucked back into our seats, Juan gripped my hand so tightly that it hurt. He was really nervous and I felt bad realizing that he must've been that much more scared when he flew to Canada all by himself. I would have gone to get him but couldn't afford it at the time.

"Why are they giving us plastic cutlery?" Juan asked when they started the food service.

"What do you mean?"

"Well, the last time I flew I got a metal fork and knife and we had real glasses and napkins." He waited for my response.

"Are you kidding me right now?" I looked at him wide eyed in disbelief.

"No, why do we have these?" He waved his plastic fork in front of my face.

"Oh my God, that's why your flight cost so damn much. I can't believe it...you flew first class! You were in the very front of the plane right?" I laughed.

"Yes."

"Well I hope you enjoyed your first class flight. I've never flown first class. This is hilarious." I was stunned that I paid for a first class ticket but even if I would've known I would've paid for it anyway.

Juan was very eager to land and as we flew closer and closer to the big mountain in Puerto Plata and over a part of the city, he eagerly pointed out the land marks.

Juan was Dominican but he was living abroad, something that could be and would be taken advantage of. He didn't care about that; his pockets were filled with money. He wanted to make an impression when he went back home and there was nothing I could do about it. We shared one suitcase and brought a second one filled with gifts and clothes for his family. They were going to get whatever they had asked Juan to bring.

I think he went overboard spending more than two thousand dollars during those two weeks, but he wanted to give to his family a taste of what he had in his new life.

We stayed on a resort because the cost difference from a flight only, compared to an all-inclusive package wasn't that much different. To have security, all the food and liquor we wanted as well as privacy, a resort was the best choice for us.

I felt like a nuisance quite often on this trip. Juan wanted to spend time with his family and friends and I felt like I was inconveniencing him. I stood out like a sore thumb and if he took me with him to some places he would have to pay double the price and so on. He just wanted to relax and enjoy himself and not have to worry about me.

I ended up on the resort by myself some of the days which I wasn't happy about but I had to let my husband enjoy being home.

When we returned back to Canada, it took us almost a year to pay back the money we had spent, and we didn't have a car.

We would walk to the grocery store down the road with backpacks.

"Why can't we just take the bus?" Juan complained every time.

"If we took the bus that would be almost four dollars each way, why spend the money when we can just walk?" was always my response.

So we walked through blizzards and sometimes rain because I couldn't justify paying eight dollars when we were totally capable of the ten or fifteen minute walk to get to and from. We needed to save every dollar possible.

I helped Juan get his license with the use of my mother's car. I spent hours helping him study the driver's handbook and a year after he came to Canada he passed the test and received his license.

It would have been easier and cheaper if he had gotten his license in the Dominican and subsequently transferred them in Canada, something I learned later.

We bought our first car in February 2007. We didn't have to walk to get groceries anymore!

Juan got a new job as a labourer with a Cuban friend and as time went on we both advanced in our careers because we worked hard at encouraging each other to do better.

Juan's Latin friends asked him to go downtown every other weekend. But only the guys could go. It was always a guy's night out and I was always cranky when Juan told me that he was going, partially because I couldn't go with him and there would be girls hitting on him, but mostly because I was still scared that something would happen to

him that would take him away from me.
It took me almost three years to stop worrying about him all the time. I however also suspected that one of the guys in his group of friends was cheating on his wife, who was also my friend. I wasn't positive it was true but I didn't want my husband having anything to do with it.
I talked to Juan about my suspicions and explained how unfair it would be if it were true.
"If you want to cheat on your wife you should leave her first" I told him.
"I would never cheat on you." Juan would say to me.
"That is what they all say." I grumbled as he kissed me goodbye.

We moved for a third time in three years during the summer of 2008 but this time to a more expensive area. It was the nicest apartment we had ever lived in. It was a new building however it seemed at that time that all of our problems and arguments originated from money. We shared a joint bank account that all of our money went into. Juan sent his family money every month and we went on vacation to visit them every year. I started feeling like his expenses were a lot more than mine. We had also been investing money into RRSPs and other things and planned on using it for a down payment towards our first house. As a result, we never had any extra money. Our second hand car broke down every few weeks and his family came into hard times with the recession just like everyone else. We tried the best we could to settle our money differences but it was very challenging.

My mother continued to spend a lot of time on the forums she had found when inquiring about other women marrying Latin men and I started getting emails from women who lived all over Canada asking me questions about marrying a Dominican.
I love helping people and so I took these women very seriously and tried my best to help them with their concerns.
One of the emails I received read like this:

"Hi Allison,
I was on a website over the weekend seeking information on marrying a Dominican and bringing him to Canada. Some of the stories I read were extremely scary. Your mother sent me your email address and said that you may have some advice or help to offer me. I think I would be happy living in the Dominican with my boyfriend but I have a son so it would be better for us to live in Canada. Your mother told me that it took eight months for your husband to get here. Is that standard or can they come prior to that time? Any advice that you can offer would be greatly appreciated as I am in the beginning stages and only wish to have positive helpful advice and not all the scary stories. I hope to hear back from you.
Thanks Sasha."

My reply was:

"Hi Sasha,
I would be happy to help you! I would like to hear your story. How did you meet and when? Unfortunately, it is standard to wait eight months after you submit your application to the Canadian consulate in Ottawa. It will usually take two months in Canada and then six in Haiti where the other Canadian consulate is. I am very relieved that it is all over now and we are finally together in Canada and doing great! Tell me a bit about yourself and what you would like to know.
Allison."

She wrote back a couple of days later:

"Thanks for the quick response.
I went down south three times in the past year on vacation and met a man who works on the resort we stayed at. He was very attentive and complimentary from the first day we met and he has shown me what it's like to be in love once again. I've been married and since divorced and did not go down south looking for love but as they say, it happens when you least expect it. I have never been this happy and I know in my heart that he is the only man for me. We've talked about me moving there or him here. We both have children and my son would have a very hard time adjusting to the school system there. I also have a house and a good job here and I have contacts that would be able to offer him work should he wish to come here. I've dated on and off in the past few years but was never able to say those three little words that have so much meaning "I love you" yet they feel so natural to say to him. I wish to know everything there is to know about being married to a Dominican. What paper work do you need before the wedding and after in order to bring him here? I am 45 years old and he is 32 however he didn't believe me when I first told him how old I was. He was like well you don't look 45 and you don't dance like you're 45, maybe 30! It has never been an issue.
Congratulations on being a role model to the rest of us starting on this exciting adventure, I'm so happy to hear a happy ending and that he is here with you and all is going very well. Thanks again for your help.
Sasha"

I responded and explained the immigration process to her. I also gave her some encouraging words and told her to be smart and not to let her guard down. It's a big deal to sponsor someone and you really want to be as sure about it as you can be.
She thanked me for my efforts and I never heard from her again.
I don't know if it all worked out for her or not but I really hope it did.

Among the many other women who contacted me this was another email I received:

"Hi there, I read your blog/comments on DR1 and was just wondering if you and your husband are still together? I apologize for being indiscreet but I have my reasons. If you can please email me back I would appreciate it."

I was curious and wrote:

"Hi there, that's okay. I like sharing my story. We are still together. He has been here in Canada with me for a couple of years now. He loves it here. It's a bit cold for him but that comes with the package. Ask me whatever you like, but tell me why you want to know. Do you have a Dominican boyfriend? They can be the best thing that will ever happen to you or they can be the biggest mistake of your life. Write back soon."

She responded the next day:

"Hi Allison,
Thanks for writing me back I greatly appreciate it. I met a man in October a few years ago and we had an amazing two weeks together. When I left I wasn't going to pursue it but he called me on my birthday and it all started. The next year I went back for a week and then again six months later when my best friend coincidentally married a Dominican. After the wedding my boyfriend took me to his home town to meet his family and we spent the week there. When I returned home we continued our relationship over the phone but I wasn't able to go back and visit for another year and by this time my friend's Dominican husband had arrived in Canada. My boyfriend and I talked about getting married the next time I went to see him but things took a turn for the worse. First with my friend's husband and then I had some personal issues. My boyfriend noticed my attitude changing towards him. I guess I asked him too many questions, which made him angry but I'm not stupid and I asked him if he was with other women. He actually came out and told me that he was, but that they didn't mean anything. I can't accept this. Although he tells me that all men in the DR are the same, it's their culture and I would never understand, I'm furious because we've had the talk about cheating and how unacceptable it is. Anyway we still talk and I still love him very much and don't know how and if I should let him go. This is a very difficult situation for me and implies a lot of responsibilities. If only there was some sort of guarantee. I would love to hear any advice you could give me.
Regards Maria"

I really felt for this girl. Long distance relationships are so hateful.

I was shocked that he actually told her the truth about cheating on her. Most people would never admit that. It took me a while to think of a response:

"Hi Maria,
Thanks for sharing your story with me. It hurts to hear about your situation. I couldn't accept him being with other women either. It's great that he is so honest but I wonder if he would be okay with you being with another man. Probably not! The Latin culture is this way a lot of the time which makes it even harder to trust them but my advice would be to not marry him right now. Maybe you could go visit him a few more times and make it clear to him that this must never happen again or it's over. I spent three years doing the long distance thing and I don't know if my husband cheated on me at the time or not, I never wanted to visit that topic because I know he would never admit it if I asked. All that matters to me now is that my husband is here with me and since the moment he arrived he has been devoted only to me. Everyone has a past and you want your man to be honest but it all depends on the situation I guess. Not all Dominicans are cheaters. You need to find out and make sure your boyfriend really loves you and only wants to be with you if and before you marry him. After you're married it's harder than you know to work through the many problems you'll have to deal with. Please let me know what happens and if there is anything else you want to know, don't hesitate to write.
Kind Regards Allison"

I don't know if the advice I was giving was good or bad but I was being as honest as I could be and never wanted people to think that it's all smiles and laughter when you marry and sponsor someone. It's a very exciting and happy thing but it is also very serious.
I received and responded to many other inquiries during this time and I also spoke with a few women over the phone who wanted the extra comfort.
I started realizing that it was not as uncommon as I believed it was to sponsor a husband.

Juan had adjusted to life in his new country very well. He didn't mind the cold anymore mostly because he worked outside and had no choice. He became more punctual and I taught him how to manage his money and to understand that just because you have money in that moment doesn't mean that it's okay to spend it on whatever you want at that moment. I drilled it into him that investing and saving was the most important thing to do with our money if we were going to have a future.
He missed his family all the time but the winter months and over Christmas was the hardest time of year for him. The only comfort he had from being homesick was remembering that he was able to support

his mother and help his family more from Canada than he ever would've been able to if living in the Dominican.

Juan and I built our first house in August 2010 which tested our relationship yet again. A house meant more responsibilities to share and disagree about.

"Let's have a big house warming party!" I hugged my husband in our empty, freshly painted living room.

"We should have a pig roast!" He kissed me excitedly. "I will get my friends to help."

It was a lot of work to plan a pig roast but we pulled it off and everyone came. We invited all the Latinos, all of our friends and some of my family.

The boys turned the pig on a spit all day and kept the fire going while the girls gossiped and helped cook the side dishes.

"Your house is so beautiful!" One of the girls said above all the chatter and music. We were outside enjoying the sunshine taking a break from the kitchen.

"Thanks for coming!" I smiled and snapped a picture of the pig.

"How long have you and Juan been together?" She waved the smoke from the fire out of her face.

"We've been together for eight years and married for five" I smiled.

"You guys are so good together." She praised me.

"Thank you, but believe me, it took a lot of time and dedication to get this far." I laughed. "Your husband has been here for how long now?" I asked.

Her husband was from Cuba and we only saw them once or twice a year, whenever there was a Latin party.

"We got married two years ago he has been here for thirteen months." She looked over to her husband who was turning the pig laughing with the other men and her eyes lit up.

We started roasting the pig at 10am and around 5pm we decided it was cooked through so the men put out the fire and lifted the pig down on a table we had and started cutting it up.

We had an open air buffet on our back deck while we listened to Merengue music in the background. It was so nice to see everyone together.

"Did you hear about Laura?" One of my friends quietly whispered in my ear as we sat down at the table to eat.

"No what happened?" I knew Laura was waiting for her husband to get approved for his Visa but hadn't heard any new information about it.

"Don't tell anyone, but she just found out through Facebook that Pedro has been cheating on her with two different girls that she knows of so far. She found pictures of him with the other women somehow on someone else's Facebook. I guess one of her other friends messaged the girls and commented about who the man was in the pictures. They told her that they met on vacation and they got together." She took a

drink of her rum and coke which added to my anticipation.
“She confronted him on the phone last night and he denied everything but pictures don’t lie, so now she doesn’t know what to do.”
“Holy that’s crazy! She can’t just believe what these girls say, it’s just a picture.” I was shocked.
“Yeah I guess, but in the pictures he has his arm around them in a pretty sexual way and they look pretty chummy. These girls have no reason to lie. They don’t know he’s married.” She lowered her voice. “Do you think Luis is cheating on me?” She looked over at her Dominican boyfriend who was chatting up another girl across the room making her laugh. “Who is he talking to?” She became irritated.
“It might be my party but I don’t know everyone here.” I admitted. “I wonder what she is going to do. That’s so awful. She might have to pull his application.” I was stressed out just thinking about it.
“He just played stupid or something. Wait, look... is she flirting with my man?”
I sighed as she got up and casually walked over to her boyfriend to check out what was going on.
I was so happy that Juan and I trusted each other completely. When he talked to other girls I didn’t care at all and vice versa. If you don’t trust each other then you shouldn’t be together, I thought as I got up still feeling disturbed by what my friend had just told me.

I went to look for Juan and found him with a bunch of his boys, laughing and joking with each other in Spanish.
He looked at me as I approached and kept his eyes on me as I walked up to him.
He wrapped his arms around me and kissed me softly. “Are you having fun baby?”
“I love you.” I hugged him.
“I love you too.” He smiled.

Prologue

Looking back now at everything that has happened to me and the other women I know, I understand how lucky I am to have a successful marriage through immigration.

I honestly believe what people say. “If you last the first 5 years of marriage you will probably be okay.” However, I also believe that it’s a different situation when you marry and sponsor someone. All the years invested in building the relationship, for some it’s only months, and then you have to factor in the immigration cost and time as well as the endless effort in teaching your spouse how to live in a *new world.*

If we would have given up on each other and divorced after a couple of years, I would have felt like my whole life had been wasted and Juan would have had nowhere to go but back to Dominican. We both knew that this wasn’t an option. Why move backwards when you can move ahead?

The first few years of marriage were possibly harder for us because we were both so young. It was probably because of the culture differences and maybe because we were both stubborn.

Whatever the reasons, we actually had countless discussions about whether we should stay together or not. There were so many things we couldn’t agree on. We had to learn how to compromise, accept each other and tolerate the things we would normally get angry about.

I tried never to look at my husband as a trophy. I tried hard not to be *too* controlling and didn’t look at our situation as him owing me because I paid to bring him here and gave him a better life.

Some people are on guard all of the time and they don’t trust their husbands at all. They ask too many questions and some women actually have justifiable reasons to be this way but others may be ruining a good thing. It is definitely hard to trust a man who has played the field like a competitive sport but if that was the case, it should’ve been recognized before the wedding and hopefully accepted as the past. It shouldn’t get in the way of the future. Trust is very difficult but is the most important element in any relationship.

The internet is proving to be a very important support system for people in these situations. I hope that I have helped the women who approached me online with their concerns. They don’t realize it but they actually helped me too! I appreciated my husband more and more with every bad story I heard and I wanted to reach out to more women and tell them that it is possible to be happy.

You have to be clever and consider all of the facts from the beginning and try not to tolerate things in the beginning of your relationship that you can’t see yourself putting up with for the rest of your life. Love is blind and it’s very easy to get caught up in.

I am no expert, that’s for sure, but I want to do whatever I can to prevent more women from getting their hearts broken. There are so many awful stories.

The word on the street *so to say*, is that Dominicans or anyone from a less fortunate country, wants to marry abroad only because of *the green card* or opportunity to have a better life in a different country. That is true for some, if not many situations, however not all.

I turn a blind eye to some of the women who are maybe twenty years older than their young attractive Latin husbands who they sponsor. Shortly after they arrive into their new country of residence, they leave their wives along with the debt they've built up from the cost of immigration and everything else acquired while helping their spouses.

It is unforgivable to take advantage of someone like this. If you find yourself in this situation, ask yourself "Does this person love me because of what I am offering them, or does this person love me because of me and who I am?"

In twenty years do you see yourself logically together? Have you thought about if they would be a good provider and what common goals and interests you share? Or did you fall head over heels for a sweet man who treated you better than any man ever has before in your whole life, and you took it farther than maybe you should have and married him? It is so easy to fall in love with a foreign language, culture and rhythm. If the first two didn't grab your attention the last one will.

Countless women from all over the world marry their Latin lovers after meeting them while on vacation and I think only a small percentage of these marriages succeed.

In the Caribbean it is somewhat tolerated for men to have a mistress and just because they move to a different country where it is not tolerated doesn't guarantee that they won't practice their old customs.

I believe that often there isn't enough time invested into the relationship before the marriage. Mostly it's because long distance relationships are almost impossible and the anguish from being apart is unbearable, but that could be a major reason why it doesn't work out in the end.

I am not sure if Immigration Canada can entirely solve the crisis of marriage fraud because many women are just consumed by love. They are blinded to the possibility that the man they want to marry might by lying about everything.

I have experienced living in the Caribbean and it might be awful to say but I sometimes don't blame these men for allowing a woman to fall in love with them, shower them with money and affection, marry them and bring them to their countries in a heartbeat.

When it's all said and done, the man is finally honest with himself and he realizes that he doesn't want to be with this girl. He just couldn't deny himself a chance for a better life when she was so confident and willing, pushing him along through the stages of their relationship. He only saw her a couple of times a year and it was fun!

It is inexcusable when men actually try to convince you with their affection and love making, telling you he loves you and wants to spend the rest of his life with you, but he really only wants the Visa.
When he gets it he might leave you standing in the airport waiting for him.
You have to realize that some people, who are poor, living in a poor country, teach themselves how to control and work their way into a better life because they have to.

If it seems like I'm trying to put a damper on the adventurous, spontaneous people out there who could fall in love in the Caribbean, I am not. That was who I was, younger than twenty years old when I fell head over heels for my Latino and I really had no idea what I was getting myself into. I don't regret any of it and I would probably do it all over again but with the same amount of discretion.

Immigration Canada is getting stricter. They are requesting more interviews and they're denying Visas to people in relationships that they feel are not legitimate. They are doing this especially because some of these women and men have turned around and blamed the government for being taken advantage of after they've spent thousands of dollars, sometimes more than one hundred thousand dollars on their lovers and then they realized that they have been deceived.
It is a legal responsibility to sponsor a spouse. You are *legally* and *financially* responsible for them for a number of years in Canada. You have to support them by law for those years and in extreme situations if they leave you and go on welfare or any type of government assistance you will have to pay for that too.
There are faults in the Canadian Immigration system, as there are in all systems however the government trusts *you* to make the right decision when you sponsor your spouse.
The government's advice to people is "if you are considering spousal sponsorship, you will want to be positively sure that the person you are marrying is marrying you for the right reasons otherwise both parties could risk being charged."

In closing, to all you single people out there, if you ever fall in love in the Caribbean be clever. Don't be naive; some people are way smarter than you think. Be realistic and don't believe everything you hear. Use your own judgment and consider all the facts and use protection!
Trust is one of the most important things in a long distance relationship so if you're in a long distance relationship, hang in there. Time might be against you now but later, that's all you will have.

I apologize if I've offended anyone. I wanted to write my story in order to give others a chance to hear a *good* story. The bad stories are mostly all people want to talk about.
I want you to know that if you take precautions and make very cautious

decisions in this situation, you will have a better chance to come out on top.
It was a good decision for me; one of the best I have ever made. Aside from all the hostility, insults, humiliation and all the lost friends along the way, it was all worth it. After all, the best things in life are worth waiting for and fortunately my husband was worth every second of it.

I hope my story inspires those who have a love for the Caribbean, and the people who live there.

Courtney Hernandez and her husband have been happily married for 7 years. They live the Canadian dream in rural Nova Scotia. They have a house, a car and an Amstaff/Lab named Maisen. They are both successful in their careers and look forward to Caribbean vacations at least once every year. In her spare time, Courtney likes to make wine and spend time with her family and friends.

www.ingramcontent.com/pod-product-compliance
Ingram Content Group UK Ltd.
Pitfield, Milton Keynes, MK11 3LW, UK
UKHW041934190726
13854UKWH00004B/1592